THE REAL READER'S QUARTERLY

Slightly Foxed

'A Dickens of a Riot'

NO.60 WINTER 2018

Editors Gail Pirkis & Hazel Wood
Marketing & publicity Stephanie Allen & Jennie Harrison Bunning
Bookshops Anna Kirk
Subscriptions Hattie Summers & Olivia Wilson

Outside cover illustration: Chris Wormell, 'The Fox', wood engraving
Chris Wormell never went to art college or had any formal training and is entirely self-taught.
Nevertheless, he has become one of the finest illustrators working in Britain today. His
illustrations, predominantly wood engravings or linocuts, are timeless, beautiful and inspiring.
For more about him and his work visit www.chriswormell.com or www.theartworksinc.com.

Inside cover illustration: Posy Simmonds, 'Office Life'

Design by Octavius Murray
Layout by Andrew Evans
Colophon and tailpiece by David Eccles

© The contributors 2018

Published by Slightly Foxed Limited
53 Hoxton Square
London N1 6PB

tel 020 7033 0258
email office@foxedquarterly.com
www.foxedquarterly.com

Slightly Foxed is published quarterly in early March, June, September and December

Annual subscription rates (4 issues)
UK and Ireland £40; Overseas £48

Single copies of this issue can be bought for £11 (UK) or £13 (Overseas)

All back issues in printed form are also available

ISBN 978-1-910898-24-6
ISSN 1742-5794

Printed and bound by Smith Settle, Yeadon, West Yorkshire

Contents

Contents

John Watson

The Slightly Foxed Podcast

The first episode of our new podcast is now available. In Episode 1, 'Kindred Spirits', Gail, Hazel, Steph and *SF* director Jim Ring meet round the kitchen table at No. 53 to remember how it all began and Veronika Hyks gives voice to Liz Robinson's article on Anne Fadiman's well-loved *Ex Libris*.

To listen, visit www.foxedquarterly.com/pod or search for Slightly Foxed on Audioboom, iTunes, or your Podcast App. Future episodes will be available on the 15th of each month, starting this December.

From the Editors

Well, this issue is our 60th, and it's making us feel a bit ruminative – emotional even – remembering the little group (four plus a baby) who sat round Gail's kitchen table, discussing an idea for a magazine that we weren't at all sure would work. The baby is at secondary school now and the original four has nearly trebled, if we count all the great people, both full-time and part-time and with ages ranging over six decades, who contribute to the production of *Slightly Foxed*.

  So once again we say thank you to you, our subscribers, who've made it all possible – especially those who took a punt on us at the beginning and have stuck with us right through. We're always cheered by your letters, and happy if we can provide an escape route to a saner, friendlier world.

One of the pleasures of editing *SF* is choosing the covers, and for this 60th issue we've commissioned a special wood engraving from the distinguished illustrator Chris Wormell. His handsome fox in classic posture seems to us to embody the lasting qualities we aim for in *Slightly Foxed*. And what a pleasure too to welcome back one of our favourite artists, Posy Simmonds, who has captured the *SF* office and its occupants in her inimitable style on the inside covers.

The author of our winter SFE is another much-loved artist, E. H. Shepard, whose delicate illustrations will for ever define the characters of Mole and Ratty and Winnie-the-Pooh. In *Drawn from Memory* and *Drawn from Life* (see p.13) he evokes in words and enchanting pictures the London of his childhood in the twilight years of the Victorian era. For anyone who was brought up on his timeless characters, these two little volumes would make a perfect Christmas present.

And yes, it's time for another of our literary Christmas crosswords, which you'll find at the end of the catalogue. Entries should be with us by 15 January 2019 and the first correct one drawn out of a hat will receive a free annual subscription. And/or you may like to consider entering our 2019 Writers' Competition. Entries this year netted us five excellent pieces for the magazine – two joint winners, one of which you'll find on p.89, and three runners-up. The competition is open to all *SF* subscribers and the winner will receive a prize of £250. Do look carefully at all the information about entering on our website www.foxedquarterly.com. Entries should reach us by 31 March 2019.

Finally, as you'll know, Jennie and the team keep *SF* well up-to-speed in all matters digital. But, for those of you who, like us, sometimes struggle to understand the world of social media, we can't resist passing on the following, which reached us via our subscriber Janet Morgan:

> For those of my generation who do not, and cannot, comprehend why Facebook exists: I am trying to make friends outside of Facebook while applying the same principles. Therefore, every day I walk down the street and tell passers-by what I have eaten, how I feel at the moment, what I have done the night before, what I will do later and with whom. I give them pictures of my family, my dog and of me gardening, taking things apart in the garage, watering the lawn, standing in front of landmarks, driving around town, having lunch, and doing what anybody and everybody does every day. I also listen to their conversations, give them 'thumbs up' and tell them I 'like' them. And it works just like Facebook. I already have four people following me: two police officers, a private investigator and a psychiatrist.

Happy Christmas!

GAIL PIRKIS & HAZEL WOOD

A Dickens of a Riot

DAISY HAY

Last year I decided that I felt like reading Dickens at Christmas. Resisting the temptation to turn to old and reliable fireside favourites, I alighted instead on *Barnaby Rudge*. It seemed a choice that would fulfil two purposes: quenching my thirst for some Dickensian delights while teaching me something of an episode about which I wanted to know more. *Barnaby Rudge* is a historical novel, one of only two such novels Dickens wrote. It was published in 1841 and was the work he planned the longest and most carefully. Yet it is rarely read today and wasn't very popular when it was published either. One contemporary critic apparently dismissed it as 'Barnaby Rubbish'.

It turns out that in many respects *Barnaby Rudge* isn't very Christmassy. Nor, however, is it rubbish. In parts it is completely terrifying, and those who like their Dickens served with a slice of Pickwickesque jollity should probably look elsewhere. Its plot is uneven, its women are nonentities, and its central character can't really carry the weight of the narrative. There's an odd five-year gap in the middle of the story, and the main historical character, Lord George Gordon, is only introduced two-thirds of the way through. However, in spite of all this, my discovery of last Christmas is that it's also amazing, unsettling and brilliant. If your test for festive reading is that a novel should grab you and not let you put it down; that it should allow you to ignore the crunch underfoot of wrapping paper and children's toys; that it should pin you to your chair so that

Charles Dickens, *Barnaby Rudge* (1841)
OUP · Pb · 752pp · £9.99 · ISBN 9780199538201

your movements are reduced to re-stocking the fire and the chocolate pile, then *Barnaby Rudge* is for you.

The novel's full title is *Barnaby Rudge: A Tale of the Riots of 'Eighty*. The 'Riots of 'Eighty' are better known today as the Gordon Riots of 1780, during which, according to the estimate of some historians, as much damage was done in London over five days as was inflicted on Paris during the whole of the French Revolution. The riots started in response to the government's decision to enact a very limited re-laxation of the civil disabilities suffered by Catholics. Under the leadership of Lord George Gordon, the Protestant Association of London mounted a campaign for repeal of this relaxation and on 2 June a crowd of around 50,000 people marched on Parliament.

Historical accounts of what happened next vary, but the general consensus is that Gordon quickly lost control of the mob he had roused as violence spread outwards from Parliament into the streets of London. All over the city the houses of Catholics were razed to the ground and individual householders were forced to write 'No Popery' on their walls in order to protect their property. In one part of London the priceless library of Lord Mansfield was destroyed; else-where a distillery was plundered until the streets ran with gin. Most famously the rioters burned down the door of Newgate prison and set all the prisoners free. Today historians tend to characterize the riots as an expression of anger against power, rather than merely the result of religious tensions. Whatever the motivation, the result was that hundreds of people were killed in the worst outbreak of public disorder since the Civil War.

Barnaby Rudge follows a loosely interconnected group of charac-ters through London's streets in the years leading up to the riots, and, in its gripping final section, in and out of the riots themselves. It opens with a group of drinkers at the Maypole tavern reminiscing about an old and unsolved murder at a nearby house, the Warren. On early inspection all this looks straightforwardly Dickensian. The Maypole is a proper Merrie England pub, with a roaring fire, a portly

The Maypole

barman and a crowd of stock regulars; and the murder is related as a grisly tale designed to make both drinkers and reader pull a little closer to the fire. But this convivial scene is interrupted by the arrival of a menacing stranger, whose presence induces gut-churning fear in several of the novel's central characters. Terror and disruption follow the stranger out of the pub and into the hearts of several of the families connected to the Warren and the Maypole, as private dramas weave in and out of an increasingly volatile public story.

In a large and untidy novel, certain individuals and pairings stand out. The barman of the Maypole, John Willet, is tyrannizing his son Joe; his sometime customer, Sir John Chester, is an equally bad parent to his son, Edward. At the Warren the Catholic Mr Haredale is doing his best to protect his niece Emma from the house's murderous history, as well as from the anti-Catholic feeling menacing their fragile peace. Across London the locksmith Gabriel Varden is the only truly cheerful character in the novel, even though his querulous wife and her maidservant Miggs (one of the novel's richest and most appalling characters) do their best to dampen his enjoyment of life. Varden's apprentice Sam Tappertit, meanwhile, has joined an underground society of 'Prentice Knights' who are busily plotting the overthrow of their masters, while his daughter Dolly is a good-hearted coquette merrily engaged in breaking the hearts of both Sam Tappertit and Joe Willet.

Moving between these families is Barnaby Rudge himself, a mentally impaired young man based on Wordsworth's 'Idiot Boy', who becomes embroiled in the riots and whose mother has more reason than most to fear the appearance of the menacing stranger at the Maypole. Barnaby is accompanied everywhere he goes by his pet raven Grip, whom Dickens modelled on his own childhood pet and who plays a small but pivotal role in his master's fate. In the final third of the novel new characters join the cast, some macabrely funny, some downright sinister. Lord George Gordon appears as a naïve religious enthusiast who is entirely at the mercy of his sinister secretary Gashford, while the Maypole's ostler Hugh takes centre stage as the ringleader of the riots. Hugh's vices, however, have nothing on those of the Newgate hangman Mr Dennis, whose pride in his profession comes back to haunt him in the final pages.

The other character to loom large in *Barnaby Rudge* is London itself – not the London of *Great Expectations* or *Oliver Twist* but rather the London of the late eighteenth century. Dickens builds a vision of the that city from his own childhood memories, and from his intimate knowledge of the old quarters and wynds he walked night after night. No one captures better than Dickens the way different worlds co-exist in London. The prosperous Clerkenwell street on which Gabriel Varden lives, for example, is just a few minutes' walk from the mouldy cellar to which Sam Tappertit escapes to plan the downfall of all apprentice-masters. The streets are lawless places at night, and an ominous sense of danger abroad tracks all who venture from their own houses after dark.

Dickens takes a great deal of trouble to remind his readers that the London of the 1770s bled in and out of the countryside much more fluidly than does their own city.

Six-and-sixty years ago, a very large part of what is London now had no existence . . . nature was not so far removed, or hard to get at, as in these days; and although there were busy trades in

Clerkenwell . . . it was a purer place, with farm-houses nearer to it than many modern Londoners would readily believe, and lovers' walks at no great distance, which turned into squalid courts, long before the lovers of this age were born.

This conjured London of old comes to life most vividly when the action moves to Newgate prison. Anyone who thinks that *Barnaby Rudge* is rubbish should take another look at Dickens's description of the storming of Newgate, which is both violent and compelling:

And now the strokes began to fall like hail upon the gate, and on the strong building; for those who could not reach the door, spent their fierce rage on anything – even on the great blocks of stone, which shivered their weapons into fragments, and made their hands and arms to tingle as if the walls were active in their stout resistance, and dealt them back their blows. The clash of iron ringing upon iron, mingled with the deafening tumult and sounded high above it, as the great sledge-hammers rattled on the nailed and plated door; the sparks flew off in showers; men worked in gangs, and at short intervals relieved each other, that all their strength might be devoted to the work.

I can't think of another description like this, in which the mob also becomes a character, a single entity with its own humanity comprised of a mass of individuals working as one. Literary critics have speculated about where Dickens's sympathies lie in *Barnaby Rudge*. Some argue that the novel's ending celebrates the restoration of law and order, others that the Newgate scenes reveal Dickens's detestation of the Georgian 'Bloody Code' that his own age had inherited. Whatever his politics, it is clear that he enjoyed recreating the destruction of Newgate a great deal. Writing to his friend John Forster of his progress he reported rather gleefully: 'I have let all the prisoners out of Newgate, burnt down Lord Mansfield's, and played the very devil . . . I feel quite smoky when I am at work.'

The combined result of all this is that you feel, when you're reading *Barnaby Rudge*, as if you'd been picked up and dropped in the middle of a country waiting to explode. Just as town and country shift seamlessly in and out of each other, so the different strands of the plot come together during the summer nights of the riots to pull you from one drama to another. Dickens was a reporter before he was a novelist and he knew just where to train his eye. He also understood exactly how to pace the action. Writing to John Landseer, he explained that his method in writing about the riots was to 'go on to the end headlong, pell mell, or they lose their effect'. Headlong, pell mell, is about right. In his second historical novel, *A Tale of Two Cities*, Dickens would perfect this way of recreating history, and there's no doubt that he takes some time to get into his stride in *Barnaby Rudge*. Once he gets there, though, the effect is electrifying, as is the experience of walking through the crowd in his shadow.

There's no denying then that there are quite a few things wrong with *Barnaby Rudge*. It doesn't have the clarity of vision of Dickens's later novels, or the iconic characters of his most famous works. Yet it makes a world and it puts you there, and it holds you in its grasp. It's a rough diamond of a book, in which you can see Dickens trying out lots of the techniques he would perfect as his career progressed. But it is not simply an overlong historical experiment or an easily dismissed apprentice work. In every page Dickens reminds us that power corrupts those who hold it as well as those who are oppressed. In the process he creates a vivid account of what happens when fathers and sons, husbands and wives and friends of different political opinions forget to treat each other with understanding and respect. And in the end it is affection, civility and friendship that triumph. What, really, could be more Christmassy than that?

DAISY HAY is currently working on a book about a group of writers who walked the dangerous streets of the London described in *Barnaby Rudge*. She is the author of *Young Romantics* and *Mr and Mrs Disraeli*.

Between the Lines

SUE GEE

The lodger has gone home to Germany for dental treatment, and I have crept into her room with a purpose. Standing on a kitchen chair, I pull out from the top of the bookshelves three little hardbacks, worn and water-stained. They date from the 1940s and '50s, though they were published decades earlier, and are bound in blue, green and yellow cloth. One is energetically scribbled on in pencil; in one I have made an early attempt at writing my name; another is inscribed by my mother: '*Not to be taken away. To be kept for the next generation!*' She was a great one for exclamation marks. My I LOVE YOU in awkward capitals, upside down at the bottom of *Now We Are Six*, is probably addressed to her, though it might be to the small round bear in the corner, wearing a waistcoat and clutching a piece of paper, for I certainly loved him too.

These little volumes are the cherished books of my early childhood and that of countless other children. In 1924, *When We Were Very Young* sold over 5,000 copies on the first day of publication; within eight weeks it had sold 40,000 more. Within four years, with the publication of *The House at Pooh Corner*, Christopher Robin, Alice and Buckingham Palace, Mary-Jane and her horrid rice pudding, Pooh, hunny and the Hundred Acre Wood had settled into the English home as if they had always been meant to do so, and it is hard to know whether it is the featherlight words of A. A. Milne or the airy 'decorations' of E. H. Shepard that everyone has ever since loved the more, so perfect was their partnership.

Ernest Howard Shepard was born in 1879, the youngest of three children. He was small – known as 'little' Shepard at the Royal Academy Schools where he received his adult training. And his memoir *Drawn from Memory* (1957), which covers 1887, the Golden Jubilee year in which he turned 8, is an account of a happy, loving child gazing up at the adult world.

Henry Shepard, his father, was an architect; his mother Jessie, daughter of the water-colourist William Lee, was musical; their milieu was one of artists, of easygoing drawing-rooms, music and song, and they gave their children a sweet-tempered domestic life, complete with outings: to pantomime, music hall, studios and private views. The house in St John's Wood was roomy and well-run, with the staff below stairs very much a part of things. And the children were close. Cyril was Ernest's great companion: any number of little incidents begin with 'Cyril and I . . .' in a brothers' world of toy soldiers, cricket, guns and steam engines. Older than both the boys was their sister Ethel, a diligent, self-possessed child, and no less charming for that, who inherited her mother's musicality and wrote spirited plays for family theatricals.

There were also the aunts. Henry Shepard's four maiden sisters lived in a house built by their father on the corner of Gordon Square in Bloomsbury. They took a keen interest in the children, scooping them up for annual summer holidays in places not so very far away: Highgate, Wimbledon, Guildford. Aunt Alicia, his godmother; Aunt Annie, an invalid; Aunt Fanny, 'by far the most energetic'; Aunt Emily, 'stout and short of breath': Ernest drew them all.

His gifts were recognized and encouraged early on, with presents of copybooks, paints and pencils. Full of energy, and the relentless curiosity of a small boy, he drew everything: the aunts; Queen Elizabeth and her knights in armour after a visit to Hampton Court; the horse-drawn fire engine racing to the scene of a raging fire at

Whiteley's department store. The joy he had from paper and pencil is evident throughout.

'The first thing I did when we were back was to rush upstairs and get out my copybook and all the pencil ends that I could find . . .' His focus is not on himself – though an engaging self-portrait springs from every page – but on his subject; and in childhood, as in his adult life as an artist, his subject is chiefly people. For that is what Pooh, Piglet and Eeyore (not forgetting Toad, Ratty and Mole, and all the rest of them) are, of course, and it is Shepard's humanity and gift for penetrating the smallest change of mood or expression that has given them their enduring appeal.

One of the many delights of *Drawn from Memory* lies in what is now the largely lost art of the caption, which in a golden age of children's literature surely helped shape the prose style of many a young writer: 'Reminded me of a respectable stork'; 'Airing my nightshirt over the gas'; 'Threw herself on a policeman'; 'Watched him cut and shape some little frogs'; 'Too shy to kiss her'; 'Cyril was sick'.

Each one raises a smile, but the 'untroubled bliss' of Shepard's childhood was to end in tragedy. *Drawn from Life* (1961) opens with the death of his adored mother when he was 10, 'a bereavement which entirely altered our family life'. The children, sent to stay with the aunts, were devastated: 'I never dreamed she *could* die.' The aunts gave them 'kindness beyond words', and when their storm of weeping was over, 'We solemnly agreed we would cry no more, for Mother would not have liked it.' Ernest, though scarred for years, was determined to justify the faith she had shown in his talent.

His father, then working as an architectural adviser to University College Hospital, had rented a studio in Gower Street, and told him he could practise in it. Students from the Slade came to buy their paints in the shop beneath it; right in the heart of London's artistic life, Ernest spent the summer holidays making his first attempts at drawing from the antique, gazing up at his father's cast of the *Venus de Milo*.

A word about his father must come here. Bereaved, grieving – he never married again – and often short of money, he managed (not without his sisters) to give his children stability and the gradual return of happiness. He was ever-present in their lives, which, after a year of living with the aunts, were taken up with a move to Hammersmith: he had found a run-down but airy and affordable house in a terrace on the river. They would be able to watch the Boat Race, always a great thing. And another important change was in view: after enduring a bullying and badly run prep school in St John's Wood (while Ethel attended Queen's College, Harley Street), Ernest and Cyril were to go to St Paul's.

A further member of the family now makes a significant appearance: Uncle Willie, Henry's brother, who had taught in the school for many years, almost certainly arranged for the boys to attend for reduced fees. Ernest was happy there. He did not shine academically – the cry of 'Ernest, *have* you done your homework?' had rung through his early childhood – though he enjoyed science. But for two mornings a week they worked in the drawing school, and here, of course, he shone. 'I drew every sort of subject, with a preference for battle scenes . . . [and] was soon promoted to a drawing board and a stool to make studies from the antique.'

In his last year, encouraged by the ambitious High Master, he successfully applied for a scholarship to the Royal Academy Schools and, encouraged by his father, began attending Heatherley's Art School on Saturdays. The school, in Newman Street, was well-established, but 'The tuition was not good and I often think I should have done better to have gone to the Slade where, under Tonks, more attention was paid to good drawing.' In addition, leaving school at 16, 'I did not consider what effect [it] would have on my general education, and I have often thought that another two years would have given me a better start in life.'

Nonetheless, in 1897 he took up his scholarship, cycling in from Hammersmith to Piccadilly, working from ten to three. And now,

after all those years of drawing, from life and the antique, Ernest was expected to paint. On holiday in Wales (the Shepards were great ones for holidays) an early landscape in oils, *A Bridge over a Trout Stream*, required for an annual prize, proved a struggle, and he did not win, though later, with Poohsticks, he was to draw one of the most famous bridges in children's literature.

Back in the RA painting studio, copying a Velázquez, he finally received a few useful words on the subject from a girl who stood watching him work. 'I think you're frightened of it,' she said. 'Try painting more thickly. The drawing's all right, but don't be afraid of going over the edges.' The speaker was Florence Chaplin, the talented granddaughter of one of the founders of *Punch*.

Ernest had been susceptible to girls from an early age, falling for pretty ones in dance classes, the daughters of family friends, any number of pantomime Principal Boys. Now, though he did not know it, he had met the love of his life. ('Your drawing is much better than your painting,' she told him on another occasion, her directness – and accuracy – a mark of her own character.) It would be another two years before he encountered her again, got to know her properly, and finally made his proposal. Both were gifted, impoverished and, eventually, overcome by their feelings for one another. The story Shepard tells of their courtship is tender and touching. Each left the RA Schools with major prizes.

The beginning of their married life, with which these memoirs conclude, lay in a very modest Surrey cottage, found by Shepard on a cycling trip. His feeling for home, nurtured in childhood, ran so deep, and doing it up for his beloved gave him so much fun and pleasure, that it is hard not to hear the voice of Ratty, waiting down the years for the artist to bring him to life, and pronounce it a capital little place.

SUE GEE and the novelist Charles Palliser have for twenty years run author events at the Stoke Newington Bookshop. Meetings of the N16 Writers & Readers group take place on the second Monday of every month: all are welcome.

E. H. Shepard's *Drawn from Memory* (192pp) and *Drawn from Life* (224pp), both including their original drawings, are available as a set from *Slightly Foxed* in a new limited cloth-bound edition of 2,000 copies (subscriber price: UK & Ireland £34; Overseas £38; non-subscriber price: UK & Ireland £37; Overseas £41). All prices include post and packing. Copies may be ordered by post (53 Hoxton Square, London N1 6PB), by phone (020 7033 0258) or via our website www.foxedquarterly.com.

From Bloomsbury . . .

ALAN BRADLEY

I sometimes think that the books that have stayed longest in my mind are those that I haven't read. As I scan my shelves, many of the titles my eyes pass over are books I read about while still at school or heard about at university; books bought in a rush of enthusiasm which faded as something new grabbed my attention.

In my salad days the two volumes of Virginia Woolf's *The Common Reader* were among the most influential. Volume 1 was published in 1925 and Volume 2 in 1932. They are collections of reviews and journalism, written while she was also creating some of her best-known novels. They cover literary criticism, character sketches and the byways of reading. I have never forgotten how enticing she made Sir Philip Sidney's *Arcadia* sound:

> We are drawn on down winding paths of this impossible landscape because Sidney leads us without any end in view but sheer delight in wandering. The syllabling of the words even causes him the liveliest delight. Mere rhythm we feel as we sweep over the smooth backs of the undulating sentences intoxicates him. Words in themselves delight him. Look, he seems to cry, as he picks up the glittering handfuls, can it be true that there are such numbers of beautiful words lying around for the asking? Why not use them, lavishly and abundantly? And so he

Virginia Woolf, *The Common Reader*, Vol. 1 (1925 · 288pp · ISBN 9780099443667) and Vol. 2 (1932 · 336pp · ISBN 9780099443674) are available as Vintage paperbacks at £9.99 each.

luxuriates. Lambs do not suck – 'with bleating oratory they craved the dam's comfort'; girls do not undress – they 'take away the eclipsing of their apparel'; a tree is not reflected in a river – 'it seemed she looked into it and dressed her green locks by that running water'.

Who could resist? Well, my college tutor could: 'Too many purple passages!' he said severely. My innocently cheeky reply at the time was that I didn't think so, but that was why I wanted to study English with people who knew better.

After three years of being taught better, I was haunted by his austerity for a long time. But the rebellious voice inside me that loved the smooth backs of undulating sentences has never entirely evaporated and came bubbling up again when I recently reopened *The Common Reader*. The delight of Woolf's essays is at least in part thanks to her own readiness to rush forward on the waves of language. It is her enthusiasm that grabs attention and leads us along the shelves, begging us to pause and open what has so long been neglected.

She has an eye for female writers, even those whom fashion and time have pushed into the shadows. Elizabeth Barrett Browning's *Aurora Leigh* had run to thirteen editions by 1873. But by the time Virginia Woolf was reading it forty or fifty years later, the received opinion she quotes from a contemporary academic held that: 'Neither education nor association with her husband ever succeeded in teaching her the value of words and a sense of form.' How much more entertainingly Virginia Woolf says the same thing:

> In short the only place in the mansion of literature that is assigned to her is downstairs in the servants' quarters, where, in company with Mrs Hemans, Eliza Cook, Jean Montgomery, Alexander Smith, Edwin Arnold, and Robert Montgomery, she bangs the crockery about and eats vast handfuls of peas on the point of her knife.

But she still reads the novel-poem and shines a light into the servants' quarters to whet our appetite:

> We cannot read the first twenty pages of *Aurora Leigh* without becoming aware that the Ancient Mariner who lingers, for unknown reasons, at the porch of one book and not of another has us by the hand, and makes us listen like a three years' child while Mrs Browning pours out in nine volumes of blank verse the story of Aurora Leigh.

Her curiosity and empathy for a fellow writer make her sympathetic to Browning's desire to create poetry out of everyday life. But she is well aware that self-parody and bathos lurk in potholes along the way. However – and this is the hook that reels us into the bookshop to buy a copy – she emphasizes that

> if she meant rather to give us a sense of life in general, of people who are unmistakably Victorian, wrestling with the problems of their own time, all brightened and compacted by the fire of poetry, she succeeded. Aurora Leigh with her passionate interest in social questions, her conflict as artist and woman, her longing for knowledge and freedom, is the true daughter of her age.

Others, whose reputations are beyond recovery, can still be a source of pleasure and delight. Margaret Cavendish, Duchess of Newcastle, is one:

> Nevertheless, though her philosophies are futile, and her plays intolerable, and her verses mainly dull, the vast bulk of the Duchess is leavened by a vein of authentic fire. One cannot help following the lure of her erratic and lovable personality as it meanders and twinkles through page after page. There is something noble and Quixotic and high-spirited, as well as crack-brained and bird-witted about her. Her simplicity is so open: her intelligence so active; her sympathy with fairies and animals so true and tender.

Or Laetitia Pilkington, who was a mere three feet two in height.

Can you imagine a very extraordinary cross between Moll Flanders and Lady Ritchie, between a rolling and rollicking woman of the town and a lady of breeding and refinement? Laetitia Pilkington (1712–1759) was something of the sort – shady, shifty, adventurous, and yet, like Thackeray's daughter, like Miss Mitford, like Madame de Sévigné and Jane Austen and Maria Edgeworth, so imbued with the old traditions of her sex that she wrote, as ladies talk, to give pleasure. Throughout her Memoirs, we can never forget that it is her wish to entertain, her unhappy fate to sob . . . Still, though her room near the Royal Exchange is threadbare, and the table is spread with old playbills instead of a cloth, and the butter is served in a shoe, and Mr Worsdale has used the teapot to fetch small beer that very morning, still she presides, still she entertains. Her language is a trifle coarse, perhaps. But who taught her English? The great Doctor Swift.

And then a little gossip is tipped in and we get an endearing glimpse of Dean Swift himself.

'Well,' said he, 'I have brought you here to show you all the Money I got when I was in the Ministry, but don't steal any of it.' 'I won't, indeed, Sir,' said I; so he opened a Cabinet and showed me a whole parcel of empty drawers. 'Bless me,' says he, 'the Money is flown.'

So she goes backwards and forwards in time, from Chaucer and the Pastons to Meredith and Hardy. Little snippets of gossip flash by, new vistas open and one is reminded of the sheer pleasure of wandering, drifting to stop at a flower here and a weed there, across the centuries of English literature.

Notoriously, Woolf doesn't write about the women on whom she herself depended for home comforts but, mostly, about those who were educated and wealthy enough to write diaries or letters. But she was very aware of the limitations society forced upon all women, both socially and physically. And how much can be gleaned from letters that will never be written, let alone preserved, in our modern, high-speed age. She was writing at a time when letters were still the main method of communication. Telephones, it is true, were around, but only for those who could afford them; they were not the ubiquitous appendages they are today. No mobiles, no texting, no Internet. Communication was measured in hours and days rather than seconds. It took time and correspondence to develop a new friendship, as is shown by her account of the friendship between Geraldine Jewsbury in Manchester and Jane Carlyle in Cheyne Walk in London. They met quite briefly at a party when Geraldine visited London, but Geraldine's determination to develop a friendship led to a steady correspondence which finally, in 1843, led to Carlyle himself suggesting that they invite her to stay.

Jane reflected that a little of Geraldine would be 'very enlivening', but, on the other hand, much of Geraldine would be very exhausting . . . She came on the 1st or 2nd of February, and she stayed till Saturday, the 11th of March. Such were visits in the year 1843. And the house was very small, and the servant was inefficient. Geraldine was always there. All the morning she scribbled letters. All the afternoon she lay fast asleep on the sofa in the drawing room. She dressed herself in a low-neck dress to receive visitors on Sunday. She talked too much. As for her reputed intellect, 'she is as sharp as a meat axe, but as narrow'.

Mrs Carlyle almost had to turn her out of the house, and while Geraldine got into the cab, her eyes full of tears at parting, Jane's were decidedly dry. Indeed she was immensely relieved to see the last of her visitor. But Geraldine continued to correspond and so the friendship recovered and deepened. You'll have to look at Volume 2 of *The Common Reader* to follow it to its sad end.

Mrs Woolf's views may not always please the reader, but they are always thoughtful and stimulating. 'How should one read a book?' is the title of one essay. Another, 'The Russian point of view', attempts to characterize the differences between Chekhov, Dostoyevsky and Tolstoy and why they each appeal so much, and in such different ways, to British readers. 'On not knowing Greek' also explores what we take from our world into reading the literature of another.

Gwen Raverat, decoration for *The London Bookbinders* (1950)

If I can see that some passages are purple, that as with Sidney, language runs away, carrying her on its back, jolting this way and that, sometimes even threatening to throw the rider, *The Common Reader* still remains an exhilarating and stimulating experience. And as she herself says:

After all, what laws can be laid down about books? The Battle of Waterloo was certainly fought on a certain day; but is *Hamlet* a better play than *King Lear?* Nobody can say. Each must decide that question for himself. To admit authorities, however heavily furred and gowned, into our libraries and let them tell us how to read, what to read, what value to place upon what we read, is to destroy the spirit of freedom which is the breath of those sanctuaries. Everywhere else we may be bound by laws and conventions – there we have none.

In retirement, ALAN BRADLEY continues to rediscover the joys of reading in spite of his education.

. . . to Buckingham Palace

HAZEL WOOD

Last Christmas I had pneumonia. I lay in bed feeling utterly miserable, listening to the sounds of sociability below. Occasionally someone came up to tempt me with a tiny morsel of Christmas food, but I couldn't eat. I couldn't read. I couldn't even bring myself to listen to the Queen – for I must admit to being a royal groupie who watched ten episodes of *The Crown* at one sitting. It was, however, a 'royal' book that marked the beginning of my recovery. One morning, I took it from the shelf beside the bed, opened it and, instead of closing it listlessly after a paragraph or two, went on reading – or rereading – until I'd reached the end.

It didn't take long – it's only 120-odd pages. Alan Bennett's *The Uncommon Reader*, which first appeared in 2007, is a gloriously funny and subversive little book about a serious subject – the importance of books to humanize us and their power to change our lives. And despite or perhaps because of its hilarity, it delivers a message just as telling as does Virginia Woolf's famous book which gave it its title.

Entering Bennett's parallel universe, we discover the Queen, alerted by the barking of the corgis, chancing upon the Westminster mobile library parked by the dustbins in one of the Palace courtyards. Mounting the steps to apologize for the row, she finds the librarian, Mr Hutchings, and a single customer, Norman, 'a thin, ginger-haired boy in white overalls'.

Having broken the ice ('Have you come far?') the Queen discovers

Alan Bennett, *The Uncommon Reader* (2007)
Profile · Pb · 128pp · £7.99 · ISBN 9781846681332

that gay Norman, who works in the Palace kitchens, is a passionate, self-educated reader, absorbed that day in a book about Cecil Beaton. Slightly at a loss now, she wonders whether perhaps she should borrow a book.

She'd never taken much interest in reading. She read, of course, as one did, but liking books was something she left to other people. It was a hobby and it was in the nature of her job that she didn't have hobbies . . . Hobbies involved preferences and . . . preferences excluded people . . . her job was to take an interest, not to be interested herself.

However, after hedging a bit ('"One doesn't have a ticket." "No problem," said Mr Hutchings.') her eye is drawn to a vaguely familiar name – Ivy Compton-Burnett (hadn't she once made her a dame?). Mr Hutchings stamps the novel and the Queen takes it away.

She finds it hard going, but returning it the following week – a good excuse to cut short a tedious briefing by her Private Secretary on a coming visit to a road-research laboratory – she decides to try again. Her next choice, Nancy Mitford's *The Pursuit of Love*, rings many aristocratic bells and is much more to her taste – compulsive in fact, and she's eager for more. And so the scene is set for a Palace revolution, in which Norman is promoted from washer-up to page boy with a special brief to keep the monarch supplied with books, and the Queen discovers an all-engrossing new activity: reading for pleasure. Before long, with Norman's encouragement and a newly acquired membership of the London Library, she is devouring the classics, enjoying poetry and even engaging with Proust.

How Bennett must have enjoyed writing this book. The Palace setting, with its hierarchies and snobberies and constipated bureaucracy, and the shrewd no-nonsense voice of his central character, allow him to take pot-shots at all his favourite targets: official jargon, literary pretension, slippery politicians, trendy attitudes – and ultim-

ately, perhaps, the infantilizing effects of Monarchy itself, with its
suburban lifestyle hidden behind the glittering façade.

Since the Queen comes to literature afresh, her judgements are
honest and down-to-earth. ('Am I alone in thinking that Henry
James needs a good talking to?' she observes.) She delights in taking
the mickey out of her Private Secretary Sir Kevin, a trendy new
appointee with a chip on his shoulder. Her crisp judgement of writers, after a sadly failed literary party at which she had hoped to
discuss their work, is that 'authors were best met with in the pages of
their novels'. And she clearly has the number of the PM, the unnamed
but easily recognizable Tony Blair, whose smug composure is rattled
when he's caught out by the Queen's Proustian clues for charades
during a ghastly weekend at Balmoral.

The Queen's new preoccupation, however, isn't popular with her
staff, who begin to notice that royal visits are not going as smoothly
as they once did. Instead of putting her subjects at ease with the usual
routine enquiries, now she is keen to know about their current reading, which leaves most of them either tongue-tied or
holding things up by enthusing at length about their
favourite books. Conversation at State Banquets falters
as Heads of State struggle to respond meaningfully to
questions about their national authors.

> 'Now that I have you to myself,' said the Queen, smiling to left
> and right as they glided through the glittering throng, 'I've
> been longing to ask you about the writer Jean Genet . . .'
>
> Unbriefed on the subject of the glabrous playwright, the
> president looked wildly about for his minister of culture. But
> she was being addressed by the Archbishop of Canterbury.
>
> 'Jean Genet,' said the Queen again, helpfully. '*Vous le con-
> naissez?*'

In the grip of this new obsession, the Queen becomes increasingly
resentful of her royal duties. She can't wait to get back to her book.

And the more she reads, the more she begins to notice subtle changes within herself. Where once she would simply have 'taken an interest' in the people she meets, now she's genuinely feeling it. She is suddenly touched by the vulnerability of those on whom she is conferring honours: 'You see, Gerald,' she confides to a surprised equerry, 'as they kneel one looks down on the tops of people's heads a good deal and from that perspective even the most unsympathetic personality seems touching . . . One's feelings are almost maternal.'

But all this caring and sharing is embarrassing and inconvenient for her staff. The Queen is no longer a figurehead, she's become a person. And as a person she's found her voice. Discouraged from reading Hardy's famous poem about the sinking of the *Titanic* as part of her Christmas broadcast – it's not thought by officialdom to be sufficiently 'forward-looking' – she still manages to surprise the assembled company at the end of a bleak Northern tree-planting when, resting on the ceremonial spade, she recites by heart Philip Larkin's poem 'The Trees' with its final line: 'Begin afresh, afresh, afresh.'

And as that clear and unmistakeable voice carried over the shabby wind-bitten grass it seemed it was not just the huddled municipal party she was addressing but herself too. It was her life she was calling upon, the new beginning hers.

I won't tell you what that momentous new beginning turns out to be, just urge you to read this deliciously funny and poignant little fable about the Queen's lonely journey to break free and find herself. Of course it's not really about the Queen at all but about a republic – the great republic of literature, 'that vast country to the borders of which I am journeying but cannot possibly reach', as she herself humbly describes it – and the winding paths and chance encounters that often lead us to discover it.

Despite co-editing *Slightly Foxed*, HAZEL WOOD feels she still has a long way to journey in the great republic of literature.

Rock, Root and Bird

JUSTIN MAROZZI

Sometimes it doesn't matter if you discover a literary classic later in life. Sometimes it can be a disaster. One can only feel sympathy for those readers who came across *Le Grand Meaulnes* at any point after adolescence. With each rereading the widening distance between one's long-lost youth and the adolescent flash and fire so brilliantly evoked by Alain-Fournier seems more and more unbridgeable. The connection is torn away in what can feel like a minor personal tragedy. Yet to read it for the first time as a 17-year-old is an unrepeatable joy.

The Living Mountain, thankfully, is a treasure that, rather like the Cairngorms it describes so wondrously, stands alone in space and time. Happening on it at any point in one's reading life brings unexpected pleasure. It is thanks to Robert Macfarlane, who has written a typically penetrating introduction to a new edition, that the book, first published in 1977 after lying orphaned in a drawer for four decades, is now enjoying a second wind. So much so that the recent, universally glowing accolades even include the claim that this is 'the finest book ever written on nature and landscape in Britain'. For Macfarlane it is 'one of the two most remarkable twentieth-century British studies of a landscape that I know'. So we are in serious territory here.

Nan Shepherd, the author of this little-known, rediscovered gem, might have choked on her hillwalker's flask of tea to read such superlatives about a book for which she was unable – or was it unwilling?

Nan Shepherd, *The Living Mountain* (1977) · Intro. Robert Macfarlane
Canongate · Pb · 160pp · £8.99 · ISBN 9780857861832

– to find a publisher for half a lifetime. When it *was* finally published, in the same year as Bruce Chatwin's *In Patagonia* and Patrick Leigh Fermor's *A Time of Gifts*, it is only fair to say that it created a modest literary ripple rather than an out-and-out splash. And yet.

Books, as we know, can have curious gestation periods and lives of their own. Nan Shepherd was known in her lifetime for a trio of novels, published from the late 1920s, and a collection of poetry, which appeared in 1934. There then followed decades of literary silence, precisely why we may never really know. *The Living Mountain* only saw the light of day four years before her death in 1981 at the age

Susie Leiper, 'All are one' from Nan Shepherd's *The Living Mountain* (silverpoint and casein paint on wood, 15x9cm, private collection, photo Anneleen Lindsay)

of 88. Until last year, when the first biography of Shepherd was published (*Into the Mountain: A Life of Nan Shepherd* by Charlotte Peacock), much of this enigmatic writer's life was a mystery, beyond the fact that she worked for four decades as an English lecturer at what is now Aberdeen College of Education.

The Living Mountain is not mountaineering literature as we have come to know it: honourable exceptions aside, thank goodness for that. There are different, more valuable thrills to be found in these pages. Those searching for the familiar fare of self-dramatizing male mountaineers slogging up cols, pioneering suicidal new routes up snow, rock and ice, and 'knocking off' summits in moments of hypoxic, hallucinating glory will be disappointed. Shepherd does not go in for that characteristically male brand of bravado. Her writing instead is marked by a gentle lyricism which unfolds across, and helps shape and reshape, this extraordinary landscape, to the point where peaks are neither here nor there. In her Cairngorms summits are mere distractions from the greater, more interesting whole.

The clue, I think, lies in the title, *The Living Mountain* – that use of the singular. I found myself captivated by this sense of the organic whole, the distillation of an entire range of mountains encompassing more than a hundred square miles into a single entity. For Shepherd, 'The plateau is the true summit of these mountains; they must be seen as a single mountain, and the individual tops . . . no more than eddies on the plateau surface.' It is an arrestingly aerial, almost other-worldly, perspective in a book which, despite its slim dimensions, offers multiple viewpoints and visions of a landscape experienced deeply and repeatedly over a lifetime. And it is not just the various aspects of the Cairngorms themselves which meld into the singular. The wind and weather, the flora and fauna, the very air itself are all constituent parts of the living mountain. 'The disintegrating rock, the nurturing rain, the quickening sun, the seed, the root, the bird – all are one.' If this may be a little too Zennish for some readers – the book ends with an overtly Buddhist flourish – it should be said that the mysticism and metaphysics are worn lightly and conveyed, like the rest of the book, in sparkling prose.

Shepherd's observational powers, expressed through a lens which moves serenely from the smallest detail to the broadest, wind-lashed panorama, announce her as a writer of real distinction. In a tripartite section on 'Life', divided into chapters on plants, wildlife and man, she marvels at the flora that somehow survives in this savage environment. She delights in 'birdsfoot trefoil, tormentil, blaeberry, the tiny genista, alpine lady's mantle', all of which look 'inexpressibly delicate' from above, though their sturdy roots below bespeak a 'timeless endurance'. There is profound physical satisfaction in walking through the 'soft radiance' of amethyst-coloured ling, kicking up 'a perfumed cloud' of pollen. She revels in the sight and smell and touch and sounds of shocking-pink moss campion, bog myrtle, pine, spruce, birch and juniper. The roots of enormous Scots firs are 'twisted and intertwined like a cage of snakes'.

Shepherd is more alive to her environment than almost any other writer one can think of. Her writing bristles with aperçus – light catching the down of a ptarmigan's translucent breast feather (a 'fugitive spindrift'); blueberry growing out of the stumps of fir trees felled in the Great War: 'a multitude of pointed flames seem to burn upwards all over the moor'. Forensic attention is given to the mystery of how running water freezes.

> But the struggle between frost and the force in running water is not quickly over. The battle fluctuates, and at the point of fluctuation between the motion in water and the immobility of frost, strange and beautiful forms are evolved.

Who has pondered so elegiacally the many sounds of water, 'the slow slap of a loch, the high clear trill of a rivulet, the roar of spate', or paused long enough to discern 'a dozen different notes' on a short stretch of burn? This is Britain's Arctic, a land of ferocious, frequently fatal storms. She records the worst one to hit the Cairngorms in fifty years, watching the great mountain mass 'eddy and sink and rise (as it seemed) like a tossed wreck on a yellow sea', flashes of rock and ice jutting through 'the boiling sea of cloud' like masts and spars as 'the sky kicked convulsively' around them.

The prose-poetry continues with the fauna of the Cairngorms. To read Shepherd on the 'mad, joyous abandon' of the swift swooping over a precipice again and again for the sheer delight of it is to recall Leigh Fermor writing on dolphins gambolling off the Peloponnesian coast in *Mani*. This is a world of white hares 'streaking up a brown hillside like rising smoke'. She muses startlingly on the swiftness of the eagle and the peregrine falcon, the red deer and the hare, wondering why grace has been added to the severely practical necessity of speed. Perhaps 'the swoop, the parabola, the arrow-flight of hooves and wings' become lovely through their obedience to function so that 'Beauty is not adventitious but essential'.

The travel writer and warrior Wilfred Thesiger used to say that it was the people, not the places, that mattered most to him. They are likewise fundamental to Shepherd, part of the living mountain, and she pays grand tribute to those wind-wizened souls who have made this wilderness their home.

Shepherd teaches us, too, to view the world with new eyes. The living mountain she contemplates with such wonder has an inside, she tells us, and this sharp but gentle contemplation of the interior finds its natural reflection in her own internal journey of discovery, enabled and framed by the mountain, 'for as I penetrate more deeply into the mountain's life, I penetrate also into my own'.

'It's a grand thing to get leave to live,' Shepherd wrote in *The Quarry Wood*, her first novel – words which now appear on the Scottish £5 note. In this, her last published work, she demonstrates how dazzlingly she used such leave as a gift for living, listening, loving, recording, discovering and, above all perhaps, for writing.

JUSTIN MAROZZI is an enthusiastic and entirely undistinguished hillwalker, which can be a challenge in north Norfolk.

Keeping Ahead of the Game

CHRISTOPHER RUSH

Most of us can respond with deep childhood memories to the line 'I'm going to tell you a story', words which we repeat to our own children and grandchildren; and this is the formula applied by the anonymous fourteenth-century author of *Sir Gawain and the Green Knight*, perhaps the greatest of Middle English poets, surpassing even Chaucer. His is a poem which appeals to the ear rather than the eye; its art is oral, and also linear in that it does not encourage its audience to flick the pages, of which there are ideally none; and although the modern reader of a Penguin Classic can do just that, it's a temptation to which you are unlikely to submit, the suspense being too full of fascination. And as you soon realize, or are asked to believe, that even the narrator himself does not fully understand what is going on but can only relate what he has been told, you readily slip into the spirit of the thing and return to childhood. Even after the Green Knight has initially come and gone, it's not clear if he is a goodie, a baddie or something in between; or if he's a ghost, a person in disguise, the Green Man or Death. Anything is possible: so right from the start

---

There are many translations of *Sir Gawain and the Green Knight* available in paperback. Simon Armitage's version (Faber, 2007 · £10.99 · ISBN 9780571223282) is grittily modern, while Bernard O'Donoghue (Penguin, 2006 · £8.99 · ISBN 9780140424539) has aimed at plain-style modern verse and achieved it, with one self-confessed loss: his version abandons alliteration altogether, whereas one has to accept that the highly wrought alliterative style is, as Armitage expresses it, the warp and weft of the poem. The original and splendid 1958 Penguin translation by Brian Stone is now only available electronically, but we can obtain second-hand copies of the printed edition.

you are in the midst of a ripping yarn.

How many know the story already? The question takes me back to my last year in primary school, when I was awarded the only literary prize I have ever won. It was for an essay 'On the Evils of Alcohol', set by the village Ladies' Temperance Association – a misnomer, as abstinence, not temperance, was their aim. The prize was *Stories of King Arthur and His Knights*, retold for youngsters by Barbara Leonie Picard. I devoured this book and was gladdened by the far-away world it created, and saddened at its dissolution. Yet curiously, by the time I re-encountered Gawain a decade later as a student, I had forgotten the drift of the story, so my enjoyment was undimmed, even though we had to translate all 2,500 lines of it from a medieval dialect that was only slightly less daunting than Anglo-Saxon.

Robert Gibbings, detail from a wood engraving to illustrate Thomas Mallory's *Le Morte d'Arthur*, 1936

But to our tale. The setting: King Arthur's court; the time: New Year's Day, with Christmas celebrations continuing unabated; the atmosphere: a delightful one, with happy, well-fed people enjoying the indoor warmth and colour of the festive season in spite of hardship and cruel weather without; a world at ease with itself and a splendid midwinter scene, straight from a Book of Hours. Until suddenly the Christmas party is gate-crashed, by a mounted knight who charges in, right up to the top table, to offer a challenge. Or is it just a Christmas game?

The knight himself is ambivalent: massive but elegant, monstrous but merry, a jovial giant; and, apart from his red eyes and golden equestrian accoutrements, suggestive of lusty youth – skin, hair, beard all green, the colour of growth, of nature; but also the colour of the dead, of devils and fairies, the otherworld, underworld, after-world which is always liable to break into a Scrooge's sleep, the skeleton at the feast. What would Christmas be without its visitants?

The rider holds in one hand a bob of holly, evergreen in winter, life in the midst of death. But beware: the holly bears a berry as red as any blood, a prickle as sharp as any thorn, and a bark as bitter as any gall; even if Mary did bear sweet Jesus Christ for to redeem us all; even so, blood and thorns and gall remind you of the cross and a cruel death. And how sure are you of resurrection? Still, the holly is offered in the manner of an olive-branch, presenting the bearer as a bringer of peace; whereas in the other hand, in spite of the soft clothes and absence of armour, he carries a huge battle axe, bristling with alternative implications.

What an opener! And there's a lot more to come. What he has to say is equally ambivalent. The tone is brusque, that of the hostile challenger, while the message itself is contradictory. He wants them to take part in a merry jest, which turns out to be a deadly test, the sort of jape involving blocks and necks and heads, and hoots of laughter. After all Christmas is just the time for quips and cranks and wanton wiles, is it not?

The game is deadly simple: he invites any knight to step up, take hold of the battle axe, and strike at his neck, while he kneels bare-headed and unresisting . . . the condition being that if he survives the blow, the striker must seek him out a year and a day later in order to receive a return blow. The challenge seems to be without a catch, and yet they all shrink from it, understandably enough – surely there *has* to be a catch? The fairy-tale year and a day simply sounds like a stay of execution, a temporary reprieve, and the outcome inevitable. Suddenly the Green Knight is, by implication, Death, and Gawain, who accepts the challenge, is Everyman, summoned to meet his end without a friend to accompany him. Nobody wants to go there. We all have to in the end, we know that, but not just yet . . .

And this is exactly how things fall out. The Green Knight submits to the stroke; his head is duly chopped off; he duly picks it up again, holds it by its long green hair to glare at the terrified gathering, sternly reminding Gawain to keep his part of the bargain; and then he leaps back headless into the saddle and gallops off, the hooves striking sparks from the flints of the floor, announcing himself perversely on departure as the Knight of the Green Chapel – the only geographical hint Gawain is given for the journey he must eventually make. And we are at the end of the first part of the four-part poem.

Part Two opens with the passing of the year: winter, the Lenten time, spring, 'softe somer', Michaelmas, the back-end days, moving into sombre November, the cycle of the seasons and the liturgical landmarks acting as an undertone of change and decay and eventual death. Gawain's day of departure to find the Green Knight is the second day of November, All Souls' Day, when masses are sung for the souls of the dead. The point could not be clearer: Gawain is a dead man; in the minds of his fellow knights he is as good as gone.

Eight weeks later, after an arduous journey, coming up from north Wales and the wilderness of the Wirral, he arrives at an oasis, the castle of Sir Bertilak de Hautdesert, and on Christmas Eve, in time to celebrate the birth of the Redeemer. It has been a penitential journey too: gentle Jesus is also Judge – of those who fail the end-of-the-world test. Testing is one of the poem's major themes. Merry Christmas then – but bear that in mind. Not that the poem thrusts eschatology in your face, but it's part of the ground bass of the ecclesiastical year – lost, alas, on most modern readers.

For now Gawain can forget all that. Sir Bertilak turns out to be an extrovert host with an amiable stunner of a spouse; his castle a second Camelot; Gawain is flooded with hospitality, conviviality and relief from the rigours of winter. God rest ye merry gentlemen.

The guests leave – all except for Gawain. The genial host won't take no for an answer. And it's no use arguing you're a man on a mission, when the host says he not only knows the whereabouts of the Green Chapel but that it's only two miles away. He'll provide a guide and they can set off at dawn on New Year's Day and arrive in time to do whatever has to be done there. Nothing, it now seems, can stand between Gawain and his destiny.

Except for the 'exchange of winnings' agreement. Sir Bertilak enjoys a joke. Let's make a bargain, he suggests: you stay in bed for the next three mornings while I go out hunting; you'll have my wife to keep you company and see to all your needs while I'm away; and whatever prize I take at the hunt will be yours on my return; and anything good that comes your way will be mine. Agreed?

It's at this point that the alert listener – or reader – will hear a bell ring. Haven't we been here before – a year ago? And didn't that contract turn out to have an unwritten clause and a darker agenda? But Gawain goes along with it and we reach the end of the second part.

Part Three occupies the last three days of the year, on which Sir Bertilak and his wife hunt their respective prey: deer, boar and fox outdoors, while indoors Gawain has nowhere to hide as the apparently ardent lady parks herself on his bed, telling him 'ye are welcum to my cors' – which, in spite of some scholars trying to pass it off as a metaphor for 'I am at your service', means exactly what it says: my body is yours. In other words, take me.

Of course, there's no steamy stuff, it's only implied; and there's comedy in Gawain's dilemma: the courtly love code insisted that a gentleman should not refuse a lady, but what sort of gentleman would dishonour his host? All Gawain can do is to beg for 'mercy'. But 'mercy' is itself in the courtly romances a euphemism for sex. So the conversation is formally flirtatious and cloaked in double entendre.

Undercutting the comedy however is something more serious. Gawain is under sentence of death. He is not the man to betray his host – under normal circumstances. But if you're facing execution in three days' time, what would be your strongest instinct – to stay pure and die a good death, or to say 'to hell' (literally) and go out happy, finish up with a final fling? In fact passions do flare up on the third morning (one of the poem's many strengths is that its hero is not the perfect knight, he is as human as the rest of us), but he holds out and, not wishing ungraciously to refuse her altogether, accepts instead another gift of 'mercy'. It's her girdle. Apart from showering him with kisses (three today, up on yesterday's two and the first day's one), all to be passed on, in the best way possible, to her husband, she offers him this item. Not a piece of underwear but a costly belt, whose true value lies not in its precious stones but in its life-saving powers: whoever wears it is safe from any assailant.

Some Christmas present! How can he refuse? He has resisted her advances but now she offers him not love but life, sweet life. And he wants to save his skin as much as the fox, to whose behaviour Gawain's is likened when on the third day he slyly keeps the girdle, while guiltily passing on the kisses as all his day's winnings. Beneath the fairy-tale surface is reality; keeping your word or keeping your life – the two don't always come into conflict but when they do you are in a cleft stick, and how you react depends on how human you are.

Next morning, the morning after the three kisses, Gawain awakes to hear the cock crow, echoing Peter's triple betrayal of Jesus. He huddles deeper under the bedcovers. After all, what was that girdle, really? Supposing it was some sort of trick . . . This is no mere Monday morning feeling; getting up to go to work on an icy morning is one thing: rising to look your executioner in the face is quite another. Gawain doesn't want to get dressed at all, but he has to go out and keep his appointment with his destiny. And so the story continues . . .

But I don't. I lay down my pen here, so as not to spoil it, except to say a word or two about the poem. We are fortunate to have it, existing as it does in a single manuscript, one quilled by a jobbing scribe and not by the unknown author who, as a devotee of an alliterative revival which did not catch on, paid the additional penalty of writing in a language which was probably considered 'dark' and 'hard' even at the time, and generally eludes even those who enjoy original Chaucer, whose language became standard English.

Fortunately there are several good translations, and though great poetry is untranslatable, for those who feel inspired to crack open a great poem, I have given details of some of these at the foot of p. 34.

It is well worth the effort and you will not be disappointed.

Not all poems, as Simon Armitage says, are stories, but this one is: a ghost story, a thriller, a courtly romance, a yarn, a morality tale and a myth, and a hymn to nature. For me the chief glory of the poem lies in those passages which contrast the formalities and politesse of court life with nature's thrilling and frightening wildness and uncompromising cruelty: Gawain sleeping out in his armour at night, half slain by the sleet; the graphic details of hunted animals, trapped, butchered, dismembered; and the cycles of the seasons with which most of us are long out of tune. This poem will bring you back into harmony with a song you may have forgotten how to sing. Above all it meets the criterion of a great work of literature: once you have read it things will never seem quite the same again.

CHRISTOPHER RUSH has been writing for thirty-five years. His books include the memoirs *To Travel Hopefully* and *Hellfire and Herring*, and *Will*, a novel about Shakespeare. His latest novel, *Penelope's Web*, was published in 2015.

Russian Roulette

ANNE BOSTON

Lionel Davidson's eight popular novels of adventure and high suspense were published sporadically between 1960 and 1994; three of them won Gold Dagger awards from the Crime Writers' Association, and Davidson received the association's Cartier Diamond Dagger award for a lifetime's achievement in 2001. Reading one of his novels is not unlike watching an extended action film like *Speed*, in which a bus full of passengers has been wired up to a bomb which will explode if the bus's speed drops below 50 m.p.h. – a genre described by one critic as a 'Bruised Forearm Movie, because you're always grabbing the arm of the person next to you'. All the same, in time his books fell out of print. Happily Faber, spotting quality, reissued all eight of them before he died in 2009, and four of the best have now once again been made available.

I met Davidson in 1994 when *Kolymsky Heights*, his last and arguably his finest, was published. He was slight and unassuming, with expressive dark eyes that widened when I showed him my early proof copy and said how much I'd enjoyed it. How did he come to be familiar with the 'howling wastes' of Siberia, virtually closed to outsiders for decades, so chillingly evoked in the book? It was all based on factual research, he said simply; he had never set foot there. He wrote a brief inscription above his signature on my proof copy, signed my battered paperback of his first novel, *The Night of Wenceslas*

Lionel Davidson, *The Night of Wenceslas* (1960), *The Rose of Tibet* (1962), *A Long Way to Shiloh* (1966) and *Kolymsky Heights* (1994) are all available as Faber paperbacks, each priced at £8.99.

(1960), smiled slyly and moved on. The inscription read 'All our endings are different!' But of that more later.

Davidson seems always to have been elusive, restless, something of a maverick. He was born in Hull in 1922, the youngest of nine children of a Polish tailor who died when Lionel was only 2. His Lithuanian mother (who was illiterate until Lionel taught her to read) moved the family to Streatham, south London. At 15 he was working as an office boy at the *Spectator* before moving to the Keystone Press. During the war he served as a submarine telegraphist, returning later to Keystone as a photo-journalist.

The Night of Wenceslas, set in Czechoslovakia, borrowed from his time working there postwar. It was an immediate success and set a benchmark for his particular forte of fast-moving adventure stories set in exotic places. Hard to categorize other than by their magic in rendering the utterly implausible entirely credible, the eight novels received high praise from other writers: Daphne du Maurier and Graham Greene likened Davidson to Rider Haggard; Philip Pullman introduces Faber's edition of *Kolymsky Heights* as 'the best thriller I've ever read'. Four of the eight were set in Israel, where he lived with his wife and children for a decade before returning to Britain. He also wrote several novels for teenagers under the pen name David Line.

His plots reveal a fecund imagination enriched by research. The hapless protagonists are plunged into ghastly predicaments – notably Charles Houston's encounters with Chinese soldiers and then a bear in *The Rose of Tibet* (his second novel, published in 1962: see *SF* no. 32). I was sorry to read in an obituary that Davidson disliked this work, because it manages to carry the improbable to Everest-like heights while remaining unputdownable. He can also be very funny. In *A Long Way to Shiloh* (1966), Caspar Laing, a brilliant, cocky young academic searching for a priceless ancient Jewish menorah, escapes from a Jordanian border patrol into Israel by paddling backwards through the gelatinous Dead Sea, stark naked and tortured by the salt water that stings his scratched body, with an ancient scroll taped to his head. Think Malcolm Bradbury crossed with John Buchan: a weird mixture, but it works.

Wenceslas, *Tibet* and *Shiloh* are tremendously enjoyable, if unsurprisingly they also show how attitudes have changed in the last fifty-odd years. Though Davidson is astute on character his women tend more to stock figures; in *Shiloh*, Laing's uncouth libido is thoroughly incorrect by today's standards. *Shiloh* is also historically interesting for having been written when Israel was still seen as a heroic young nation, before the Six-Day War and long before Gaza, behind its monstrous barrier, became Israel's running sore.

Davidson's last book, *Kolymsky Heights*, set in the Cold War, is more serious than the early novels and in it his storytelling reaches its peak. It had the misfortune to be published just as the Soviet Union was collapsing, which reduced its impact at the time. But today, with the rise of Putin's Russia and the cooling of East-West relations, its theme seems prescient, as advances in genetic science designed to benefit mankind are increasingly open to commercial and military exploitation.

The novel centres on a quest, a one-man mission to reach a contact in the remotest part of Siberia in an era when foreigners weren't welcome. Aside from the problem of disguising his tracks across immense distances in lethal cold, this individual has to find an underground research station so secret that it officially doesn't exist, which is buried in the permafrost somewhere in that alien land of falling whiteness, of ice and darkness. There he must obtain top-secret information from a heavily guarded source before making his way out by a different route to the West.

At 480 pages, the book is a long one for what could be classed as an 'entertainment', but it never feels over-extended, and the apparently simple linear structure is deceptive. Putting it to the test for a second time, I found that the ferocious narrative pace had lost none of its pull; yet the compulsion to read faster is slowed by the dense web of material detail, all essential to the interlocking plot.

The first section deals with finding the only man who can tackle the job and persuading him to do it. A professor of genetics in Oxford is approached through devious, encoded means by an unnamed Russian biologist who urgently needs to contact a third man known to them both. At issue is the body of a prehistoric being – not a mammoth but a young woman, found perfectly preserved deep in a crevasse – and its uses to science.

This third man is Johnny Porter, a Gitksan Indian from British Columbia, a freakishly gifted linguist with degrees in biology and anthropology, who has also studied native languages in Siberia. Porter is researching the claims of Canadian tribal people cheated of their birthright by the perfidious British; his suspicion of state authority is confirmed by his succinct negative to an early approach. Then satellite photographs detect a fire at the Siberian research station which reveals its hidden contents and increases the urgency of the situation. Something in the images, and the messages, works on Porter to change his mind.

Whoever saw the 2015 Faber edition of *Kolymsky Heights* through to print must be a fan, for several maps have been inserted discreetly in the text, minus page numbers and far enough from the narrative context to avoid giving away clues. So now you can track Porter's impossible journey around and across the icy vastness of northern Asia, and marvel at the mass of detail that authenticates his zigzagging itinerary. In Tokyo, the spooks supply him with his first identity – each disguise must be effective enough for him to embed himself in a tough job and leave no suspicions hanging over his departure. The pigtailed Korean seaman must work his passage northwards on a tramp container ship making its last navigable Arctic voyage of the year before the ocean freezes over. The bosun – a malevolent bully bent on breaking him – is one of the attendant risks.

Then after immense detours, and now disguised as a bald Siberian Chukchee truck driver, he must double back to fill in at the Tchersky Transport Company, thousands of miles to the east. Heavy trailer trucks haul freight from the port to its mines and power stations and industrial settlements along the frozen rivers which are Siberia's roads in winter. The claustrophobic hard-living communities huddled above Siberia's subterranean mineral wealth, and their casual racism towards native Siberians, are brought vividly to life. Aside from his workmates, he has women to convince: his flatmate's girlfriend, large, pale, blonde and eager, and an alarmingly intelligent medical officer who is over-interested in his health and his tribal background.

Somehow the fantastic mesh of narrative threads holds, averting a chain of disaster and increasing the suspense. How to steal a bobik – a tough little jeep built for sub-zero conditions – as a possible means of escape? (This bit is ingenious even by Davidson's standards.) How to locate the research station, find his way in and escape if his cover is blown? . . . At which point, reaching the final pages, I return to the author's inscription, for my proof copy reaches an ending different from the one that Davidson wrote for the final published version. I therefore have the rare privilege of a choice between the two. Porter's survival depends on it . . . which is it to be, this time?

ANNE BOSTON is a writer and editor and the author of *Lesley Blanch: Inner Landscapes, Wilder Shores.*

Incorrigible and Irresistible

SUE GAISFORD

Towards the end of my first year at university, I discovered the library. It took a while to navigate, but after a week or two, I wandered into the Special Collections department, watched over – if memory is to be relied upon – by a woman of obvious authority. She explained that she guarded all the old and rare books but she agreed to let me look around.

The major find that day was a cookery book. It contained some basic recipes, the most memorable of which provided instructions for preparing pork, which ran as follows: 'Take a Pigge. Smite off its head. Doe it in a faire Potte untill it be done.' It was pretty old, that book, and magnificent in its way, though the smiting could give one pause.

The next discovery was an eighteenth-century collection of the poems of John Wilmot, Earl of Rochester. On our course we were studying Rochester, as published in the Muses Library edition, and while we were certainly impressed by the rage and ingenuity of his satires, most of us had fallen slightly in love with the limpid beauty of his lyrics – especially 'Absent from thee I languish still' and 'All my past life is mine no more'. It was a little mysterious that this early collection should be kept under lock and key but, as I was briskly informed, this was an unexpurgated and obscene book, definitely not

Jeremy Treglown (ed.), *The Letters of John Wilmot, Earl of Rochester* (Blackwell, 1980), is out of print but we have obtained a handful of hardback copies in good condition. To order one please either telephone or email Anna Kirk in the office (020 7033 0258 · anna@foxedquarterly.com).

suitable for impressionable undergraduates. And, actually, would I go away now and only come back with written permission from my tutor? That is, if I really needed to return.

I was scared of my tutor, with reason, and decided to let the matter drop. However, curiosity piqued, I looked more closely at the little book of poems we had been set, and noticed odd remarks such as, 'This poem has been excluded from the present edition at the request of the Publishers.' Still, there was a lot going on at the time, and it was hard enough to keep up with the essays and the carousing demanded by student life. Rochester settled on the back burner.

Where he simmered. The next big discovery was an article by Vivian de Sola Pinto, about Alexander Bendo. This is how the story goes. Rochester was a protégé and close friend of the restored king Charles II, but he was incontinent in his habits. On his death-bed he confessed to having been continuously drunk for five years in those courtly days, and he certainly indulged plenty of other appetites. Charles was in no position to condemn his womanizing but Rochester's way with a lampoon could verge on *lèse-majesté*. He is famous, for example, for the lines 'We have a pritty witty King, whose word no man relies on. He never said a foolish thing, nor ever did a wise one.' Though Charles languidly replied that it was quite true, for his words were his own but his actions those of his ministers, trouble was brewing.

It was in the early hours of 25 June 1675 that Rochester and a gang of his rowdy pals came reeling into the Great Privy Garden at Whitehall, where a learned Jesuit had set up some glass dials, or chronometers, for the science-loving king. Then, according to Aubrey, 'dash, they fell to worke', and smashed them all to atoms. This really could not be tolerated, and Rochester had to go. He left the court.

At about this time there appeared on Tower Hill the impressive figure of Dr Alexander Bendo, wearing an old green gown, a huge beard and a massive chain, apparently given him by the King of Cyprus 'for doing a Signal Cure upon his Darling Daughter, the

Princess Aleophangina, who was painted in a Banner and hung up at his Elboe'. A copy of his long and elaborate hand-bill survives, in a memoir by one Thomas Alcock. It is magnificently outrageous. It lists every ailment imaginable, from scurvy and green-sickness to obesity, rotting teeth and 'all sorts of distempers, Malladies and Complaints whatsoever', all of them curable by the great doctor's medicine. This was brewed in an 'old boyling Kettle, of Soote and Urine', seasoned with brick-dust, asafoetida and sweat, along with ashes, lime, chalk, clay, old wall, soap and indeed anything that came to hand.

Also offering certain dubious value-added services to ladies of a delicate disposition, Dr Bendo did a roaring trade and attracted enormous crowds. And then, quite suddenly, 'the hungry court could no longer sustain her drooping spirits' without Rochester, writes Alcock, and he was summoned back, making 'the Quickest Voyage from France that ever man did'. He was at Whitehall, 'in Splendor, dancing in a Ball', the very next night. As for Dr Bendo, he was never seen again.

You have to warm to the man: such reckless ingenuity, energy, bravado – and such wonderful poetry. The only child of a mercurial cavalier general who had fought for Charles I, he had inherited the earldom at the age of 10 and gone to university at 12, before spending the best part of three years on the Grand Tour. At 17, back in England, he hired a coach-and-six and attempted to abduct Elizabeth Malet, a desirable heiress, as she travelled past Charing Cross. Two years later, she chose to marry him after all. They had four children, but his health was never strong and his life so hectic and debauched that the venereal disease he'd contracted when still at Oxford caught up with him and, after a last-minute conversion, he died, probably of tertiary syphilis, on 6 July 1680 at the age of 33.

Nowadays, his poems are readily available in all their startling frankness of style, intention and language. But much of his work was deliberately destroyed soon after his death, when his rigorously puritanical mother discovered his memoirs, and was so horrified that she ordered everything burned, the whole trunkful. Byron, 144 years later, suffered a similar posthumous fate. These bonfires are less serious than the destruction of the great Library of Alexandria – yet who can tell what marvels, what insights, what scurrilous tales went up in flames? Some of Rochester's private papers, however, survived, and it is in these intimate, personal letters that you feel closest to the mercurial, profound, scatological, paradoxical, passionate, uxorious, philandering, wickedly clever fellow that he was.

Jeremy Treglown's edition opens with the blast of war. The first letter, to his mother, is dramatically headed 'From the Coast of Norway amongst the rocks aboard the *Revenge*, August the 3rd'. To show repentance for the failed abduction of Elizabeth (and to get out of prison) the teenage Rochester had volunteered to go to sea and to serve with Pepys's patron, the Earl of Sandwich. The plan was to trap some richly laden Dutch ships in the harbour at Bergen. It went disastrously wrong and the two friends who sailed with him were both killed, 'with one shott, just by mee', though he was himself unscathed. He had had a pact with one of them that if either should die, he would return to give evidence of an afterlife. This did not happen. He never forgot this moment, understandably enough. It was 1665, the year of the great plague, when 'scarce a soul was left alive': death was never far from his, or anyone's thoughts.

Annoyingly, after that dramatic piece of reportage, he never dated his letters: the sequence becomes a matter of well-educated guesswork. Happily, his wife managed to keep many of hers from the flames. They begin in a spirit of intimate tenderness: 'Madam, if it were worth any thing to bee belov'd by mee, you were the richest woman in ye world . . . there is left for mee, noe pleasure but in yr smiles, noe life but in yr favour, noe Heaven but in yr Love.' Later, during his long affair with an actress, they become more brisk and businesslike, but then they resume a tone of deepened and affectionate respect, until, towards the end, comes the famous letter that begins "Tis not an easy thing to bee intirely happy, but to bee kinde is very easy and that is the greatest measure of happiness . . . you have practis'd that soe long that I have a joyfull confidence you will never forget it . . .'

Before this, his wife had been treated to an absurd mock-philosophical discourse on 'Heroick resolutions in woemen', a wager from Newmarket 'I'le hould you six to fower I love you . . .', a pained, thoroughly disingenuous enquiry as to what in his behaviour could possibly have caused her offence, and a splendid dispatch, as from a monarch sending gifts via an ambassador, to his daughters: the enclosed doll is 'the very person of the Duchess de la Vallière, dried up and pined away to a very small proportion by fasting'.

Another woman who kept her letters safe was Elizabeth Barry, the actress who also bore him a daughter and whom he claimed to love, though he seems not to have treated her particularly well. These are short notes, often passionate, sometimes obscure, always urgent, never signed. One begins 'You are stark mad, and therefore the fitter for me to love' and they all breathe an immediacy of emotion that mocks the intervening centuries.

Yet it is with Henry Savile, his best friend, that he really seems to come alive, and their correspondence, both sides of which survive, shows him at his most unguarded. They shared a love of wine: 'Oh that second bottle, Harry, is the sincerest, wisest, most impartiall downright Friend we have'. They also shared a destructive passion for women – their exchange on the subject of VD sweatshops in Leather Lane is particularly rich in black comedy – and an avid interest in court affairs. Savile knew all the gossip and shared it generously, though such was the intricacy of the often salacious and occasionally incestuous affairs he relays that, despite Treglown's painstaking researches, they are as impossible to unravel as a tangled skein of wool.

At the end of his life, and to the great comfort of his pious mother, he seems to have undergone a religious conversion. His friends were sceptical, but the last two letters, both written to clerics, suggest that it was indeed genuine. Like Dives in the parable, he longs to warn 'all my friends and companions to true and sincere repentance today, while it is called today, before the evil day comes and they be no more'. As for himself, he suggests that, so unforgivable were his many sins, he might be smuggled into Heaven in disguise. Perhaps he was.

The university library still holds that old copy of his poems in their Rare Books section, though more recent, unexpurgated editions are readily available on the open shelves, in all their bawdy rage: they still have the power to shock, even now. Apparently that briskly businesslike cookery book has disappeared.

SUE GAISFORD is a useful jobbing journalist, who has written for most of the broadsheets and a selection of the more genteel magazines. Currently she reviews for the *Financial Times* and is on the judging panel for the Authors' Club Best First Novel Award.

A Modern Pied Piper

MAGGIE FERGUSSON

It's some time since I visited Michael Morpurgo in his riverside flat in Fulham. When we were working together on a book about his life I came here often, watching the tide rise and fall, and listening to the seagulls cry, as Michael reminisced. Now, a few years on, the place seems unaltered, and so does Michael. He's still warm and welcoming, quick to smile, and with the deep courtesy that perhaps harks back to his days as a Sandhurst cadet. Only his voice has changed. It has deepened, and it sounds strained.

In 2017, Michael was working on two books, each of them very personal to him. The first, *In the Mouth of the Wolf*, was based on the life of his uncle Francis Cammaerts, who served with immense courage in the SOE during the Second World War, and who was decorated with the DSO, the Légion d'honneur and the Croix de guerre. The second, *Flamingo Boy*, also set during that war, in the Camargue in southern France, centres on an autistic boy, Lorenzo, growing up on a farm on the salt flats when the Germans come to occupy the region. Michael has a teenaged grandson who is autistic, and Lorenzo is directly drawn from him – his need for routine, his love of repetition, his intensity and sweetness. 'For years and years, children like this were put away, hidden from sight,' says Michael. 'Yet these people cast a great light into other people's lives because there is something elemental about them. The child that is in each of us is very visible in an autistic child.'

Michael Morpurgo, *War Horse* (1982), *Why the Whales Came* (1985) and *Kensuke's Kingdom* (1999) are all available as Egmont paperbacks. *Private Peaceful* (2003) is available as a HarperCollins hardback.

In November, the two books both well under way, Michael headed out to Ypres for a centenary commemoration of the Battle of Passchendaele. 'It was an amazing event. The Cloth Hall was lit up with extraordinary images of old soldiers. I had to retell the story as an old man looking back on how it had been to go to war.' He was speaking to thousands of people, but his voice kept letting him down. Back in London, he was diagnosed with cancer of the larynx. There was an operation, followed by radiotherapy. 'I cancelled everything for six months.'

Well, almost everything. For most of us, recovering from cancer would mean taking leave of absence from work and putting our feet up. But for Michael it's very hard to stop. Ever since he was a schoolboy, he has packed into an average day what most of us would manage in a week. In an early love letter, his wife Clare told him how much she loved his 'six selfs [*sic*]'. He's a writer, of course, but also an entrepreneur, whose charity, Farms for City Children, has given more than 100,000 inner-city schoolchildren a taste of what it's like to live and work on a farm. He's a performer, who feels most at home on a stage. And he's a crusader, who uses his fame to help him fight for the causes he holds dear. He couldn't down tools completely without going into a decline.

One thing he was certainly not going to cancel was an appointment at Buckingham Palace to receive, alongside Ringo Starr, a knighthood – though as it turned out it was an oddly underwhelming occasion. 'I was slightly disappointed that they didn't say, "Arise, Sir Michael." You know when you go to a school prize-giving it's celebratory – people clap, there's some laughter, there's a lovely atmosphere. I was hoping it might be like that. Instead, everyone sat in absolute silence – it was like church, like the C of E at its most dour.'

Nor was he going to turn down opportunities to write. As the radiotherapy started, he received two irresistible offers – the first to write a novella based on Raymond Briggs's *The Snowman*; the second to translate Saint-Exupéry's *Le Petit Prince*. 'So I got the bit between my teeth, and wrote and wrote and wrote.' As the radiology machines at the Marsden whirred and clunked around him, he concentrated hard on words and stories: 'I think it was the best way of recovering.'

For generations of children, Michael Morpurgo has been a kind of Pied Piper. No one is sure exactly how many books he's written, but there are over 150 of them, and they are said to have sold, in total, more than 35 million copies. Many have become classics – *Private Peaceful*, which follows a First World War soldier through the last night of his life before he is executed for cowardice; *Kensuke's Kingdom*, the story of a small boy washed up on an island in the Pacific; *Why the Whales Came*, set in the Scilly Isles in 1914.

And then there's *War Horse*. One evening in the late 1970s, Michael walked down to the Devonshire farm, Nethercott, to which he and Clare have welcomed inner-city children for over forty years. In the yard, he spotted a lad of about 8 leaning over the stable door talking to a horse. He'd been warned by his teachers that this boy was acutely shy and liable to take fright if asked a question. And yet here he was chatting fluently to a horse who seemed, in turn, to be listening. Watching them, Michael had an idea. He would write a novel set in the chaos of the First World War and narrated by a horse, Joey, who would witness the horror from both sides of the trenches. The rest is history. *War Horse* became a stage play which ran for eight years in the West End and has now played in eleven countries to over 7 million people. In 2011 it was released as a Spielberg film.

What is it about the two world wars that keeps drawing Michael back? Both are beyond the scope of his memory, and yet the Second World War changed his life forever. In 1945, when Michael was 2, and his father, Tony Bridge, was still away serving in the armed forces, the suave, clever, bullying Jack Morpurgo walked into his mother's life and seduced her away from her husband. Though they went on to have two children together, Michael's mother Kippe was racked with guilt for the rest of her life. When she died in 1993, Michael says, she was convinced that she had 'failed in the eyes of God'. Michael is a naturally buoyant character, but the batsqueak of grief that runs through almost all his work has its roots, perhaps, in Kippe's anguish.

From what age, I wonder, does he think children should be exposed to sadness in literature? 'I don't know the answer to that, but I've got a feeling that before the age of 9 they won't understand it and may indeed be traumatized. It's vital that they shouldn't be. But there's a big "however". I think it's fine that children grow up knowing the wonderful and glorious things, but they have to understand that there's evil in the world, and in each of us.' He tells the story of how, in 1910, the editor of *The Times* asked readers to answer the question: 'What's wrong with the world?' And G. K. Chesterton wrote back, 'Dear Sir, I am.' 'He was right,' says Michael. 'If we keep pointing the finger at others, we'll get nowhere.'

You might infer from all this that Michael, at 75, is something of a tortured soul – but you'd be wrong. Naturally upbeat, he is a doting father, grandfather and great-grandfather, who found his star early and has followed it with extraordinary devotion. 'It's a wonderful thing,' he says, 'to count your blessings. I do it more and more. I've lived to this point in good health. I've had happiness and contentment, done what I wanted to do, lived in comparative peace. It's an embarrassment of riches. Providence has smiled on me, that's for sure.'

Our hour together is drawing to a close. I'm aware that children up and down the country would have paid good pocket money to have had this time with Michael – and I'm aware that he needs to rest. As he leads me to the door, speaking perhaps more to himself than to me, he tacks on a final reflection. 'Yes,' he says, 'I've been very, very lucky. I've had a superabundance of joy.'

MAGGIE FERGUSSON is literary editor of *The Tablet* and literary advisor to the Royal Society of Literature.

Histories of the Soul

CHRISTIAN TYLER

When Bob Dylan won the Nobel Prize for literature in 2016, the world was intrigued. Dylan himself wondered exactly how his songs related to literature. The Nobel committee's explanation, that he had 'created new poetic expressions within the great American song tradition', seemed to satisfy most people. (The laureate later quoted his literary influences as *Moby Dick, All Quiet on the Western Front* and the *Odyssey*.)

A more interesting choice for the prize, however, was the previous year's winner, Svetlana Alexievich, a Belorussian journalist. This was odd, not because she was a journalist – although it is unusual for journalists to aspire to 'literature' – but because hardly a line of what Alexievich writes is her own.

Her books consist almost entirely of other people's words, which is why the Nobel committee described them as 'polyphonic'. What Alexievich does is to tape long interviews with chosen subjects, record group conversations and make notes of random remarks overheard in the marketplace or on the bus. She then edits the material and stitches it together. She is not the first to use this technique. The late

---

Svetlana Alexievich, *The Unwomanly Face of War* (1985) · Trans. Richard Pevear & Larissa Volokhonsky · Penguin · Pb · 384pp · £12.99 · ISBN 9780141983523; *Boys in Zinc* (1991) · Trans. Andrew Bromfield · Penguin · Pb · 304pp · £9.99 · ISBN 9780241264119; *Chernobyl Prayer: A Chronical of the Future* (1997) · Trans. Anna Gunin & Arch Tait · Penguin · Pb · 304pp · £9.99 · ISBN 9780241270530; *Second-Hand Time: The Last of the Soviets* (2013) · Trans. Bela Shayevich · Fitzcarraldo Editions · Pb · 704pp · £14.99 · ISBN 9781910695111.

Studs Terkel collected the stories of 'ordinary' Americans, and oral history has become a recognized discipline. But she is certainly its most powerful – and political – exponent.

By getting people to describe the seismic events of their own times, she aims to counter the official lies of the Soviet state and uncover the truth of what it did to its people for seventy years. Following the recent publication in English of her first book, *The Unwomanly Face of War* (the Second World War), we now have translations of all four of her major works. The other three are *Boys in Zinc* (the Soviet invasion of Afghanistan, 1979–89), *Chernobyl Prayer* (the nuclear reactor disaster of 26 April 1986), and *Second-Hand Time* (the collapse of the Soviet Union).

Each book required years of work and hundreds of interviews recorded on literally miles of audio tape. Alexievich was not interested in conventional responses, the kind of thing people say to journalists when they are shy, afraid of controversy or anxious to please. Since this was Russia, she had also to overcome the inhibitions imposed on her witnesses by a lifetime of subservience to the state, not to mention their deeply felt patriotism. She waited hours, days and weeks until they were ready to open up.

Her interviews were 'like probing scar tissue', she said. The men, especially former soldiers, tended to stick to the official version of events. Some were hostile, angry that this young woman should question their sacrifices for the Motherland. Former Party bosses would ring up to berate her – and end up agreeing to tell their own stories. Women were generally more confiding and would reveal to Alexievich things they had never told anyone else. The truth is sometimes too much to bear, re-living one's past too upsetting. And we, her audience, can sympathize: these stories of violence, loss and betrayal are painful to read, more shocking than anything a fiction writer could dream up. Once the floodgates of memory are opened, her witnesses are more eloquent than any novelist could make them.

These histories of the soul, as Alexievich calls them, are built up like portrait paintings. Each piece of testimony adds a layer to the canvas. They are litanies of suffering, repetitive but mesmerizing. And what emerges is a remarkably coherent picture. Even when, as in *Second-Hand Time*, the narrators fall into two camps – those who regret the collapse of the USSR and those who rejoice at it – the sentiments on each side are consistent, a guarantee of their essential truth.

Born in Ukraine in 1948, Alexievich grew up in what is now Belarus. There as a child she had overheard the women of the village – there were few men left – talking about their dreadful experiences during the Nazi invasion. It was this that prompted *The Unwomanly Face of War*, the first of her 'documentary novels' (and the only one of the four whose English translation is not entirely convincing). Women's role in the Great Patriotic War had been glossed over for decades. And when it was retrieved, it was sanitized. This

'About a million Russian girls served at the front'

sanitized version is the one the women would give Alexievich, at least while their husbands were in the room. The men did not trust their wives to tell their own stories.

About a million Russian girls, mostly volunteers, served at the front where they were generally accepted as comrades, and issued with men's clothes and boots too big for them. Some later became famous as snipers or tank crews. The unsung heroines were the nurses, teenagers who crawled repeatedly over the battlefield under fire to drag back wounded men, dead weights twice their own. Fear of death was not as bad as having to wear men's underpants, says one. Another confesses that her greatest fear was 'losing my beautiful legs'. Women found it more terrible to kill than men did, and had more to fear from capture: often they were summarily shot.

By the time they were sent home to be women again, their hair had turned white, their periods had stopped and they could not bear to look at the colour red. Some took years to recover and marry. They were not sought out by men they had served with, who wanted pretty, peacetime wives.

Boys in Zinc (a reference to the metal coffins in which casualties were sent back to Russia) is an indictment of war, the horrors witnessed by the young conscripts and the grief of mothers who have lost an only child. We hear what death on the battlefield really looks like. It's nothing like the movies, says one survivor. A soldier shot in the head can run for half a kilometre crazily chasing his own brains as they stream from his skull. Mothers describe the trauma of bereavement. What exactly lies inside that zinc coffin they cannot see and are not allowed to know. They had been assured that only sons would not be sent to Afghanistan, and would now never trust the state again.

Falsely described as a brotherly mission to build socialism, the war was conducted behind a fog of secrecy and ineptitude. Casualty numbers and war-grave locations were concealed while survivors were treated with fear and contempt. (I once met an embittered Afghan war veteran at a hotel bar in Leningrad who, in reply to my innocuous question, pulled a gun on me.) The mistrust created by the Afghan campaign is said to have been a proximate cause of the Soviet Union's collapse. All the pride and patriotism created by the victory over Hitler at Stalingrad was dissipated.

Chernobyl saw the ultimate betrayal of the people by their leaders. Not only did the nuclear reactor fail – an unthinkable failure of Soviet technology – but the plant's management failed to report the truth of what had happened. When they did, the high-ups in the Kremlin found the knowledge too great to bear. It was easier to pretend that everything was under control: so for twelve hours they refused to evacuate the people living under the radiation cloud.

Typically, Alexievich says none of this herself. She lets the people tell their own story. And the first story is the heart-rending account of a young wife from Pripyat, pregnant with her first child, whose husband went out in his shirtsleeves in the middle of the night to fight the fire on the reactor roof. She followed him to the radiation hospital in Moscow where he and his firemen colleagues were taken, bribed her way inside and was able to hold him until he died. Her baby, a little girl, was born prematurely and died of radiation poisoning within four hours.

The heroism of the firemen at Chernobyl, their pride and sense of duty, was in stark contrast to the cynical incompetence of the government. The men were oblivious to their lack of protection, which even if it had been available would not have saved them. When the army arrived, the place looked like a war zone. (Some residents thought world war had broken out.) But the soldiers were fighting a war against an invisible enemy. As one says, you did not die on the battlefield, only later when you got home.

Chernobyl was a true nightmare. The one place in the world where people felt safest – their home – was now the most dangerous place to be. Apart from the black puddles, everything looked the same as before. But everything – the house, the garden, the forest, the wild animals, the household pets – was now deadly poisonous. No wonder many of the old people simply refused to believe it and preferred to stay in this mutant world of the living dead, watching the soldiers search for clean earth in which to bury poisoned earth.

If *Chernobyl Prayer* is the most eloquent of the four books, *Second-Hand Time: The Last of the Soviets* is the most penetrating. It goes to the heart of the question which so puzzles us in the West: after everything they have suffered in the last hundred years, why do so many Russians regret the end of the Soviet Union?

Alexievich paints a vibrant collective portrait of *Homo sovieticus*. Brought up under Communism, he lives now under capitalism. In the past, he suffered poverty, bereavement and betrayal, dreading the knock on the door. Yet he had hope. 'We were people of faith,' says one interviewee. That faith was dashed when, after a brief interval of democracy, society suffered from the rampages of raw capitalism and material greed epitomized by a new dictator and his tame oligarchs. There was plenty to buy in the shops, certainly, but the prices were beyond reach. Russia became a country in which a coalminer and his family could be murdered for a stereo player. Migrants from the Caucasus or central Asia, formerly respected as Soviet citizens, found themselves subject to racial abuse and maltreatment in Moscow, the city they once regarded as their capital. If old Communist hardliners hated the new regime, many of their anti-Communist children were disillusioned too.

Second-Hand Time is the best insight into modern Russia you will read. But is it literature? It's hard to see why not. Svetlana Alexievich has discovered a powerful way of writing history. Her reality is magnified by the dignity and eloquence of history's minor actors – by their tears and silences as much as by their words. Her characters prove to be larger than life, their stories as dramatic as any novel. This journalist has used reportage to do work which, before her arrival, fiction alone was deemed capable of doing. Nowhere is human nature more exposed to our view than in her pages.

CHRISTIAN TYLER wrote a weekly interview column for six years during a thirty-year career at the *Financial Times* of London. He knows how hard it can be to get people to open up.

Whatever Happened to Elizabeth Jenkins?

NIGEL ANDREW

When she died in 2010, at the astonishing age of 104, the novelist and biographer Elizabeth Jenkins was all but forgotten, her name known only to a few aficionados, her books mostly long out of print. And yet, in her day, her reputation had been up there with the other distinguished Elizabeths of mid-twentieth-century fiction, Bowen and Taylor. What happened?

I had never heard of Elizabeth Jenkins myself until a chance conversation with a bookseller friend. He told me he had just sold one of her books and was pleasantly surprised to find that she was still being read. Elizabeth who? I asked, and he gave me the basics. Since then I have found out – and read – much more, and discovered for myself what a very fine novelist she was.

A literary career that spanned eight decades began soon after she left Cambridge. While still an unpublished author working on her first novel, she was invited to dinner by Virginia and Leonard Woolf, and duly received the usual Bloomsbury treatment – taken up and made much of, then frozen out and humiliated. Though Virginia did praise that first novel, in somewhat patronizing terms

---

Elizabeth Jenkins, *Virginia Water* (1929), *Brightness* (1963), *Dr Gully's Story* (1972), *A Silent Joy* (1992) and *The View from Downshire Hill* (2004) are all out of print but we can try to obtain second-hand copies. *Harriet* (1934) is still available as a Persephone paperback (320pp · £14 · ISBN 9781903155875) as is *The Tortoise and the Hare* (1954) as a Virago Modern Classic (288pp · £8.99 · ISBN 9781844084944).

('a sweet white grape of a book'), Elizabeth was so embarrassed by it that she sought out and bought up all the copies she could find. (It was called *Virginia Water*, published in 1929, and it does indeed seem to have disappeared without trace.) However, Victor Gollancz was sufficiently impressed to offer her a three-novel contract. Elizabeth Jenkins was on her way.

Over the coming decades, a stream of well-received novels and equally well-received biographies poured forth. Several of the biographies – of Jane Austen (Jenkins was a founder of the Jane Austen Society), of Elizabeth I, Lady Caroline Lamb and others – remain quite easily available to this day, but the novels, though they often went into several printings, are mostly much harder to find. In part, no doubt, this was a matter of changing fashions – Jenkins's novels generally inhabit an upper-middle-class milieu, and she strongly disapproved of the social changes that came about in the Fifties and Sixties. Things might have been different if she had been more of a self-publicist – or any kind of a self-publicist – but she was not. Held back by her diffident nature, she did little to further her career, shunning all publicity and self-promotion (in today's literary world she would have sunk like a stone). Happily, however, those novels were not entirely forgotten. One of them – *The Tortoise and the Hare* (1954) – was rediscovered by Carmen Callil and republished as a Virago Modern Classic, and another, *Harriet* (1934), was later reissued by the excellent Persephone Books.

The Tortoise and the Hare was the first Elizabeth Jenkins novel I got my hands on, and I was not disappointed. It chronicles the break-up of a marriage – a familiar enough subject, but handled with rare imaginative flair and originality. Imogen is the beautiful, sensitive young wife of Evelyn Gresham, a handsome, brilliant and successful barrister with a very high opinion of himself and a strong sense of entitlement, neither of which his compliant wife has done anything to dent. The Greshams have plenty of money, a big house in Berkshire and a place in town, and a standard of living that might make today's readers blink in disbelief. But are they happy? Of course they're not.

As the story unfolds, Imogen begins to realize just what is going on between her dazzling husband and the wildly improbable, and therefore easily dismissed, 'other woman', a tweedy, frumpy pillar of village society, spinster, wearer of ludicrous hats, but wealthy, capable, knowledgeable in practical affairs and strong-minded. It is in those last attributes – all of which Imogen lacks – that Blanche's fatal attraction lies. Imogen looks on in helpless agony – and, worse, in full awareness that she is collaborating in her own suffering.

There is an element of autobiography in *The Tortoise and the Hare*. Elizabeth Jenkins, a beautiful, sensitive woman herself, wrote it after being dumped by the love of her life, a married man every bit as distinguished as Evelyn Gresham. She was fatally attracted to such men, and they recur in her novels – as do sympathetic but frail victim figures. And victims don't come any frailer than the helpless title character of *Harriet*, Jenkins's second novel, which in 1935 beat Evelyn Waugh's *A Handful of Dust* to win the Prix Femina Vie Heureuse.

Harriet is a chilling read – indeed one of the most harrowing novels I've come across. Based on a real-life Victorian murder case, it tells of a young woman being starved to death by members of her own family eager to get their hands on her inheritance. The worst of it is that the young woman, Harriet, is a 'natural' (we would now say she has 'learning difficulties'). Her mother has raised her with care and affection, and all is well until a handsome and entirely ruthless fortune-hunter sets his sights on her, woos and marries her, and takes her away from her protective home.

What follows is almost too painful to read – painful not only in the details of Harriet's ordeal but in Jenkins's horribly convincing depiction of the growth, in those supposed to be looking after her, of an ability to regard her as something less than human, something whose suffering and fate are a matter of complete indifference. A contemporary review described this novel as 'like a cold hand clutching at the heart' – and that is no overstatement.

There is nothing of the cold hand in the novel that Elizabeth Jenkins always named as her own favourite – *Dr Gully's Story* (1972). This, too, takes its inspiration from a real-life Victorian murder case – the sensational and still unsolved Charles Bravo murder. However, there is no mention of Bravo until more than three-quarters of the way through, and the murder itself and the ensuing inquests don't happen until the closing chapters. The focus is firmly on the fashionable society physician James Gully (who finds himself a suspect in the Bravo murder), and on his feelings and experiences. Jenkins builds up a rich and compelling portrait of a fascinating, successful man – yes, the Evelyn Gresham type again, but additionally blessed with a peculiarly mesmeric presence.

The real subject of the book is less the murder than the passionate love affair that develops between Gully and his beautiful, rich and very much younger patient, Florence Ricardo (later to be Florence Bravo). The course of this superficially unlikely romance is traced with such imaginative insight that it becomes entirely believable and involving. Jenkins creates around Gully and Florence a world rich in intricate detail, a densely Victorian, over-furnished, hyperabundant world of *stuff* – and of servants, ever present, ever vigilant, ever gossiping – in which the principals are obliged to live their lives, while trying to keep their love affair secret. It is, of course, a doomed romance, and when it ends much of the heat goes out of the novel, though the subsequent account of the murder and the inquests is fascinating enough in itself.

One of the most striking features of Jenkins's novels is their sense of place: the riverside locations of *The Tortoise and the Hare*, Victorian Cheltenham and suburban London in *Dr Gully*, the grim rural setting of Harriet's ordeal, all are potently evoked by a writer who really does set her scenes. In *Brightness* (1963), the setting is the tight-knit Home Counties town of New Broadlands, set on a high ridge, its earliest houses 'built in the Edwardian era by a community of high-minded cranks' (we all know places like that).

Brightness is a curious novel, the first three-quarters seeming to be a fictional study of parenting, good and bad, of youthful rebellion and delinquency and the 'generation gap'. The author's loathing of 'progressive' thought – apparent in the background of *The Tortoise and the Hare* – comes to the fore here, in the portrayal of a frightful old humbug with the splendid name of Mortimer Upjohn, and, more especially, in the withering depiction of the *nouveau riche* Sugden family. The Sugdens are bringing up their late-teenage son with a toxic combination of unrestrained indulgence and non-existent discipline – with predictably loathsome results.

By way of contrast, we are given Una Lambert, a widow with a beloved son who is a credit to her firm but loving upbringing. As the novel goes on, a strain of theological speculation enters the picture, and the reader begins to wonder what kind of book this is – anti-progressive satire, a study of parent-child relations, a reflection on the nature of faith? – and where it is going. Then, suddenly, we find out exactly where it has all been going – towards a shocking and tragic event that changes everything, and puts all that came before in a wholly new perspective. This is a very bold way to shape a novel – as bold as the long delay of the murder in *Dr Gully* – but Jenkins, I think, pulls it off.

Her last novel was *A Silent Joy.* Though published in 1992 – her eighty-seventh year – it is set in 1957, among a still prosperous and servant-attended upper middle class. Once again, a strong-minded and distinguished man – an elderly retired judge – is at the centre of things. The novel is a rather schematic study of three kinds of love: the deep, disinterested affection of the judge for the young daughter of a dead friend; the naked lust of said friend's widow for a dodgy wheeler-dealer; and the sweetly conventional love of a young couple (older daughter of said friend and cousin of another friend). It is also a portrayal of the terrible effects of easy divorce – in 1957! The plot is a little lumpy and the characterization uneven, but there's always something there that keeps you reading, some scenes and moments when things come fully alive and remind you just how good Elizabeth Jenkins could be.

There are more of her novels out there waiting to be rediscovered and read. I like to think they are the kind of books that might turn up in jumble sales, or even elude the hawk-eyed valuers who monitor charity-shop donations these days. I'm certainly keeping my eyes peeled.

Elizabeth Jenkins continued writing almost to the last. A memoir, *The View from Downshire Hill* (2004), was published in her hundredth year. Downshire Hill in Hampstead was where she lived, in a Regency house that her father bought for her in 1939. She furnished it with good Regency furniture, picked up for next to nothing after the war, but could barely afford to heat a few rooms. Because of the furniture, she recalled, 'people assumed I was comfortably off, instead of being very hard up'.

Her small, hunched figure was a familiar sight on the streets of Hampstead for many years, but the distinguished and gifted author that was Elizabeth Jenkins had all but disappeared. When, in 1983, Virago issued a promotional booklet with pictures of all the Modern Classics authors, she was the only one of whom no portrait could be found. Instead, she appears in the leaflet as an outline head filled with a blank space.

Having survived twenty-two years at the *Daily Mail*, NIGEL ANDREW is now happily retired and spending more time with his eclectic blog 'Nigeness: A Hedonic Resource', reviewing, and writing a book chiefly about seventeenth-century church monuments.

In Search of Unicorns

VICTORIA NEUMARK

Did you ever yearn to live in a magical world? One where a unicorn is glimpsed in a wood, monkeys do housework and a big black cat takes messages, and where there is also, reliably, steak and kidney pie for lunch, honey for tea and cocoa for supper?

That's how my sister and I spent one summer, lost in the comforting world of Elizabeth Goudge's children's books. We were quite young – maybe 13 and 9. Our parents were fighting all the time, screaming and sulking. Most summers we trailed round European cities following my father's lectures at medical conferences, being plunged into high culture while all we longed for was to repeat our one holiday on a British beach.

It was far otherwise in Goudge territory, twinkling with exquisitely English landscapes, cosy as a quilted sampler. Whether she is describing a young child climbing slippery rock steps from a sea cave or uncovering the glories of a tangled garden in Devon, she is one of the only modern prose writers to capture the spirit of the seventeenth-century mystic Thomas Traherne:

> The corn was orient and immortal wheat, which never should be reaped, nor was ever sown. I thought it had stood from everlasting to everlasting. The dust and stones of the street were as precious as gold: the gates were at first the end of the world.

Elizabeth Goudge, *The Little White Horse* (1946) · Lion Hudson · Pb · 224pp · £6.99 · ISBN 9780745945781. *Linnets and Valerians* (1964) is out of print but we can obtain second-hand copies.

The green trees when I saw them first through one of the gates transported and ravished me, their sweetness and unusual beauty made my heart to leap, and almost mad with ecstasy, they were such strange and wonderful things . . .

Like Traherne Goudge was an ardent Anglican. But although religion can be an oppressive presence in her adult novels, in her children's books it manifests itself merely as a sense of embracing safety. One of her obituaries quoted Jane Austen's famous line from *Mansfield Park*, 'Let other pens dwell on guilt and misery.' Her fictional world is devoid of malice, which is why it was such balm to our childish spirits. Loyalty, kindness, affection, the wonder of nature, the smells of good, plain English cooking, a hot bath and clean clothes, the appealing personalities of pets: these are the things she celebrates. In Goudge's children's books, to use Louis MacNeice's phrase, there is 'sunlight on the garden' and the equation always comes out.

The Little White Horse – winner of the 1946 Carnegie Medal and one of J. K. Rowling's favourites – is set in the mid-nineteenth century. Recently orphaned young Maria Merryweather and her governess Miss Heliotrope arrive at Moonacre Manor, a paradisal demesne hidden behind a rocky wall somewhere in the West Country and home to her cousin and guardian Sir Benjamin. He welcomes her with beaming benevolence, and his huge dog Wrolf (or is he a lion?) gives his approval. The castle is idyllic: books on the shelves, the neatest little tower room and a bed with lavender-scented linen for Maria, daffodils blooming in the sheep pasture, and steak and kidney pudding for dinner provided by the irascible but affectionate Marmaduke, Sir Benjamin's diminutive cook and housekeeper.

The little white horse, the emblem on the family crest, is seen only when all is right. But all is not right. Maria senses sorrow and anger over ancient quarrels. Even Miss Heliotrope has a sad past. When sinister men from the dark woods threaten the pastoral peace of the

Moonacre Manor, by C. Walter Hodges

estate and try to kidnap Maria, the great lion-dog Wrolf races to her rescue.

But what is the terrible hidden secret? Riding Wrolf and helped by the huge black cat Zachariah and a charming shepherd boy called Robin, Maria embarks on a dangerous quest to find a missing talisman ring. It is then that the little white horse – or is it a unicorn? – is glimpsed in a wood, a blessing on the quest. When ancient enemies are finally reconciled, and the ring restored to its owner, courage and honesty are still needed to right past wrongs and reunite Robin's mother, Loveday Minette, the thoughtful provider of that lavenderscented linen, with Sir Benjamin, to whom, it turns out, she had once been engaged. They had fallen out over horticulture, but as Loveday now says: 'Don't waste hate on pink geraniums.' The ending is suffused with happiness.

Goudge's own life was to my mind a sad one, though she, in her autobiography *The Joy of Snow* (1974), does not characterize it as such. Born in 1900, the only child of loving parents, she spent an idyllic childhood in the then isolated Somerset countryside around

Wells and later at Ely in the Fens. She was sent away to school and then to art college in Reading. When her father became Regius Professor of Divinity at Oxford, her mother's ill health thrust the shy young woman into acting as her father's hostess, which she found unbearably painful. She started to write, drawing on her stays with her mother's much-loved Guernsey family for her adult novel *Island Magic* (1934). Her father was surprised – 'What a lot you have done with a little,' he commented.

Crippling depressions plagued her, though she also enjoyed growing success, creating a series of novels based on Ely (the Torminster books) and on Guernsey (the Island books). The family evolved a *modus vivendi*, whereby mother and daughter spent summers in a small Hampshire cottage and endured winters in Oxford. When her adored but somewhat remote father died in 1939, mother and daughter found a new cottage in Devon.

Here Goudge's writing flourished. She wrote more than fifteen novels, plays and books of short stories, made many friends and enjoyed travelling. However, after eleven years of increasing illness, her mother died and she suffered a breakdown. Friends rallied round, found her a cottage in Oxfordshire and a young companion-housekeeper and gardener, with whom she shared the fun of owning dogs. Her religious faith was a lifeline as was this platonic relationship, which lasted for thirty years, until Goudge's own death in 1984.

Linnets and Valerians (also called *The Runaways*, 1964) was written in this final phase. It is one of the most perfect of Goudge's books. While their military father is off serving the Empire in Egypt, the four Linnet children escape from their grandmother's gloomy custody and run wild on the moors with their dog Absalom. But as night falls, their adventure seems less enticing. They chance on a pony and trap full of provisions parked outside an inn, scramble in, stuff themselves, and let the pony take them home to its master. He, it turns out, is none other than their uncle Ambrose, a humorous vicar with a strong sense of justice and an owl on his shoulder, who takes them in. And luckily, there are still sausages for supper.

The story mixes just the right amount of mundane detail with a magical conundrum. Lady Alicia lives nearby, in a house with an overgrown garden, a housekeeping monkey named Abednego and a black servant called Moses. The house is a fascinating warren of rooms and relics of Lady Alicia's husband, lost on an exploration in Egypt, and her son, mysteriously abducted. But there are strange tensions in the village which, it turns out, is under a nasty spell. We meet the poisonously sweet and witchlike shopkeeper Emma with her evil cat Frederick who can swell to panther size, and her ally, Tom Biddle, the menacing landlord of The Bulldog pub. And who is the mysterious hermit on Lion Tor?

The children decide to set things right, with the help of the man-servant Ezra and a wondrous colony of bees (not to mention extra helpings of ham and ginger biscuits). They are vividly drawn: sensible Nan, practical and wilful Robert, sensitive Timothy and sturdy baby Betsy – perhaps the siblings Goudge wished she had had. They go where they are not meant to go, on to high moors and into hidden rooms.

The Linnets, by Ian Ribbons

One of the most touching episodes in the book is one in which the monkey Abednego snatches Betsy's doll, Gertrude. Lady Alicia tells him to return it and he weeps. Betsy demands it back, but then hesitates. She thinks of her father saying goodbye to her, Lady Alicia mourning her lost son, and now the monkey's grief.

Three times now this strange thing had touched her. She was well aware that her feeling for Gertrude was not this thing, but something far less admirable, and looking up into Abednego's face she fought a battle inside herself with the thing that it was, a sort of grabbing thing, and then she held Gertrude out to him. 'You have her,' she said.

However, Betsy does not become a saint. She is a normal 'not outstandingly unselfish child'. Goudge's compassion for her characters is always rooted in this everyday realism.

A wonderful double dénouement features both a detailed undoing of the instruments of black magic and nail-biting chases over moorland, alive with weather and tense with emotion. I'll let you guess who the hermit turns out to be and who returns from Egypt. The heart-warming reunions which end the book are marked with cloudless skies.

This world, where even the baddies turn out to be 'quite nice' and Frederick reverts to normal cat size, where only children can unknot the bizarre tangles caused by adult scheming, entranced my sister and me. We only had an old cocker spaniel, but we loved to imagine ourselves riding the lion-dog Wrolf triumphantly through orchards and meadows, as Maria does in *The Little White Horse*. We never confronted a witch, but we felt the justice of throwing books of spells and wax effigies pierced with pins into a cleansing fire, as in *Linnets and Valerians*.

'As this world becomes increasingly ugly, callous and materialistic it needs to be reminded that the old fairy stories are rooted in truth, that imagination is of value, that happy endings do, in fact, occur, and that the blue spring mist that makes an ugly street look beautiful is just as real a thing as the street itself,' wrote Goudge. This message still speaks to me. Let's stop hating each other over pink geraniums and enjoy sharing sausages for supper.

VICTORIA NEUMARK lives in north London but enjoys frequent excursions to magical realms in the company of her two small granddaughters.

Grave Expectations

RICHARD PLATT

Some people bring wine to dinner. Some bring dessert. My friends bring books, which is, I suppose, why they're my friends. One night, a 'friend' – I use the term loosely – cast a cloud over my life of unmolested tranquillity by presenting me with *The Quincunx* by Charles Palliser. (A quincunx is a group of five objects arranged so that four form a square and a fifth sits in their centre, as on a dice. I had to look it up too.) A master of the soft sell, he simply said, 'Got this at a jumble sale. It's kind of Dickensian. Right up your street.' Then, rather than handing it to me, he placed it on a table and backed away, as if he had lifted a family curse by passing it on to the innocent.

The Quincunx is 'kind of Dickensian' in the same way that the Taj Mahal is kind of a nifty tomb. Even the name of its central character, John Huffam, is lifted from Palliser's great inspirer, Charles John Huffam Dickens, but so to describe *The Quincunx* is almost to belittle it. At more than twelve hundred pages, perhaps half a million lovingly conjured words, it is as long as anything penned by Dickens, with a wheels-within-wheels complexity that Dickens, Wilkie Collins and Conan Doyle together could not have bettered. (Thankfully, there are genealogical charts, maps of early nineteenth-century London, a glossary of over a hundred proper names, and even a note on currency.) In addition, Palliser paints his characters with a subtlety of touch and linguistic exuberance that would have made Dickens glad to call them his own. Here we meet Mr Pentecost:

Charles Palliser, *The Quincunx: The Inheritance of John Huffam* (1989)
Penguin · Pb · 1,248pp · £16.99 · ISBN 9780140177626

His face, which wore an expression which I can only describe as one of indignant good humour, was red-cheeked and adorned by little half-lens eye-glasses above which bristled a pair of very bushy eyebrows that gave his physiognomy an expression of permanent surprise. His appearance did not efface but recorded the history of his dressing: a neckerchief carelessly tied, stockings ill-matched, and the act of shaving ill-completed. His stained and patched coat was covered in a fine powder and when I knew him better I understood that this was because of his habit, on becoming passionately eloquent on a subject as he often did, of throwing rapid pinches of snuff in the direction of his nose so that it flew about him like a golden mist. He wore an ancient wig which somehow always contrived to get turned round so that the queue hung over one ear, impairing the tenuous dignity of his appearance still further.

With its lush stylistic narrative, linguistic precision, long, flowing subordinate clauses, so sadly uncommon in this age of drab, staccato, Hemingwayesque prose, *The Quincunx* would have sent Henry James off to burn his unpublished manuscripts in quiet despair.

The blurb on my copy states that the novel was twelve years in the writing, and I can believe it. It is a multi-family multi-generational saga swirling around a lost will, a stolen codicil and John Huffam, a mollycoddled, self-centred child who enters life unaware that he may be the heir to a fortune, and that the death of both him and his mother, a beautiful, kindly, fragile milksop of a woman not unlike David Copperfield's Dora, would allow relatives of doubtful virtue, most of whom are unknown to him, to retain their vast inherited wealth, which is rightly his.

We meet Our Hero first at about the age of 5, and, seeing the world through his eyes, are given the missing pieces of the family story only when they are revealed to him, as he sheds the naïvety and ignorance of his childhood. There are also occasional chapters that provide us with a glimpse of the Face of Malevolence lurking in the shadows.

Our journey begins with an interview between Equity and Law, who will later become better known to us but who are introduced as allegorical figures, much like Ignorance and Want standing beneath the robe of the Ghost of Christmas Present. We are immediately plunged into the world of Regency England:

> Let us imagine that we are standing, on a wintry afternoon some years ago, in the west-end of Town. The dusk thickens, rendering even gloomier that great prison-house of fashionable society, so that all those grim and lofty streets and squares seem in the gathering mist to be riding at anchor like so many aristocratic Hulks designed for the detention of Society and its transportation to the waste shores of fashionable boredom. The grimmest and gloomiest of all of them is Brook-street.
>
> The grimmest and gloomiest of all the houses in Brook-street (which is, in point of fact, where we are) is one whose brightly-painted escutcheon over the street-door proclaims its aristocratic pretensions, as do the lofty and blank windows which gaze upon the opposite side of the street with a kind of grimace of fashionable hauteur.

TUTA ROSA CORAM SPINIS

Palliser's knowledge of the look and feel of the streets of London seems as bottomless as if he had accompanied both Dickens and Henry Mayhew on their endless walks through the metropolis. Indeed every aspect of early nineteenth-century England is meticulously and often viscerally described: the hierarchy, duties and rivalries of servants in a London townhouse, the sometimes benevolent and often predatory wretchedness of the poor, the bestial living conditions of insane asylums, the predawn arrival of the grocers in Covent Garden, and even the sewers, in some of which, as we rake through the muck and inky blackness in search of lost coins, we must tread carefully around the occasional fetid corpse, and beware the collapse of decaying brick and mortar beneath our feet, as it is of Roman antiquity.

We will receive lessons in the laws of inheritance and the language of heraldry, encounter the world of Fagin and Bill Sykes, meet body snatchers, prostitutes, murderers, thieving property speculators, conniving investment bankers (pardon the redundancy) and members of the Court of Chancery. We will shiver atop the mail coach from Yorkshire to London, having escaped a school drawn directly from Nicholas Nickleby, and be betrayed, after tantalizing foreshadowings, by almost everyone who presents himself as a friend. Our journey will conclude, most fittingly, with a chase on a dark and stormy night, a clandestine marriage, and murder in the ruins of an ancient family chapel.

The entire narrative is constructed with the precision of a Bach fugue, every passage so precisely crafted, so interdependent, as to appear indispensable: five sections, each for one of five families, each section composed of five books, each book of five chapters. Like any perfectly crafted work of art, literary or musical, nothing is superfluous and nothing is left out. A beggar who is turned away from the door will reappear hundreds of pages later. A ladder seemingly left by accident (but are there any accidents?) will be used for a burglary. A boy who on a warm spring day is taught to hold his breath and swim under water will one day save the life of another boy, and his own, with this newly acquired skill. As the Punch and Joan impresario Mr Silverlight explains, 'The purpose of a work of art is that Man may trace [the design that underlies the universe] and find the pattern . . . In any novel I collaborated upon everything would be a part of the whole design – down to even the disposition and numbering of the chapters.'

The leitmotiv of *The Quincunx* is the interplay of Chance and Design – do we perceive Design in our lives, or merely impose it? – underscored by the recurrence of those Dickensian coincidences that

Dickens's detractors so often deride as 'contrived', yet which occur in real life every day, but the foundational theme is greed: how it twists, degrades and ultimately destroys everything it touches, even the innocent, and how it so clouds the minds of men that they come to see their most heinous acts through an indestructible rose-coloured glass of self-justification. Like so much of Dickens, it is a cautionary tale. There are even hints in the final pages that Our Hero, having vanquished Evil at last, will himself succumb to the moral anaesthesia which so often accompanies vast wealth, and soon forget the few people, still alive, still struggling to survive, and but for whom he would not have prevailed, or even survived.

The Quincunx is literary art of the highest calibre. I almost wrote 'literary ventriloquism', but the narrative voice is so eerily uncanny, so numinous, that it feels more like channelling. The pressure of seemingly endless conspirators to defraud or murder John Huffam and his mother brings them closer to the edge of destruction with every page, and brought me to the edge of my chair. This is the only book that has ever made me hyperventilate. It was the best of times; it was the worst of times. On the night I wanted to finish reading *The Quincunx*, I glanced up at the clock beside my chair, which was striking eleven, and closed the book, trying to catch my breath. I had to get up the following morning for work at 4.30. If I went to bed I knew I wouldn't sleep (it would not be my first sleepless *Quincunx* night), but my mind was tiring, and if I didn't get to bed I'd regret it in the pre-dawn hours. However, if I made some tea, I could finish the book by 4 a.m., in which case I'd be a cripple all the next day. I made the tea.

RICHARD PLATT has practised his own literary ventriloquism, voicing C. S. Lewis in *As One Devil to Another*, and Henry David Thoreau in a one-man stage show, *Ripples from Walden Pond*. He is now at work on a play involving G. K. Chesterton and Oscar Wilde. See www.RichardPlattAuthor.com.

Kinsey Makes a Difference

FRANCES DONNELLY

There are authors' deaths, announced casually on the radio, that provoke an involuntary cry of loss. The recent death of Sue Grafton, author of the alphabetically themed Kinsey Millhone detective novels, was one such. How could you not mourn a writer with whom you'd kept company – and 25 books – for 36 years? An added sadness was that she would not now complete her task of a book for every letter of the alphabet. We had had *Y Is for Yesterday* (2017) and awaited, confidently, *Z Is for Zero*. Except that now it won't be. 'In our family', said one of her daughters, 'the alphabet now ends with Y.'

I first read her in 1982, a year which, coincidentally, saw the introduction of two giants of female private-eye mysteries. Sue Grafton's Kinsey Millhone made her bow in *A Is for Alibi* while Sara Paretsky introduced V. I. Warshawski in *Indemnity Only*. I discovered there was another more painful connection between them: both writers' childhoods were shaped by their mothers' alcoholism. For Sara Paretsky, childhood was a life of domestic drudgery as the main carer for three siblings and a martinet father. For Sue Grafton, aeons of neglect and an absent father allowed her to work her way unimpeded from Nancy Drew to Raymond Chandler. Her early writing career was spent in television. To write her way out of it, she turned back to her first love, detective fiction.

I say detective, not simply crime fiction, because to purists the distinctions between crime, mystery and detective fiction are finely

---

Nineteen of Sue Grafton's Kinsey Millhone Alphabet novels, from *A Is for Alibi* (1982) to *Y Is for Yesterday* (2017), are available as Pan paperbacks at £8.99.

calibrated. In her autobiographical *Kinsey and Me* (2013) Grafton pays her dues to her mentor, S. S. Van Dine who, in 1928, first laid down the rules for detective fiction. Self-evidently, he says, there must be a detective detecting, and the 'I' of the narrative must be assumed to be revealing all the information they know. The murderer must be someone who has been visible throughout the plot – no new characters are allowed to turn up fifty yards before the finishing line like marathon cheats. And the solution must have its roots in the present or past life of the victim. Armed with these stern but fair injunctions Grafton spent five years writing her first Kinsey Millhone.

It's hard to convey how completely shocked I was by it – for one simple reason. At the end of the book *Kinsey kills the murderer.* She not only owns a gun but also uses it. I was fully up to speed with women who solved crimes while knitting small fleecy garments from a safe distance, and who relied on the police to handle violence. But there is all the difference in the world between being the person who notices when a neighbour's milk bottles aren't taken in and suspects foul play, and being a woman who hangs up a shingle announcing her intention of spending her working life in the company of – among others – the marginalized, the dishonest, the unstable and the downright psychopathic. In her autobiography Grafton goes some way to explaining why this choice of protagonist appealed to her:

> The post-war Private Eye – Philip Marlowe, Lew Archer – spoke strongly to me. He was a character I recognized and was drawn to. War had unleashed him. Peace had brought him home. He carried our rage. He championed matters of right and fair play. At the same time he violated the very rules the rest of us were forced to embrace.

This somewhat ambiguous moral position spoke deeply to our heroine. Kinsey believes in having the guilty brought to account but she's comfortable with bending the rules. Admirably tidy in her housekeeping, her accounts up-to-date and bills paid, in pursuit of justice she is distinctly off-piste. She is a fluent and convincing liar. She has mastered reading documents upside down on desktops. She carries a set of door picks and uses them. To justify her presence, she carries a bogus clipboard. To justify this behaviour, she has the bedrock conviction: I don't like people getting away with murder.

Not that a private detective's life always involves violent crime. Far from it. The bread-and-butter work is serving writs, chasing up spouses and checking the validity of insurance claims. But between these mundane tasks come the stories that will lead to mayhem, and often bloody mayhem. Nothing gives me greater joy than an opening paragraph from either Chandler or Grafton. Invariably it is a fine day – we're talking southern California here – and they're sitting idly at their desks, waiting for someone to employ them. Like Mrs Culpepper in Grafton's short story 'Between the Sheets' (1986):

> I squinted at the woman sitting across the desk to me. I could have sworn she'd just told me there was a dead man in her daughter's bed. Which seemed a strange thing to say in such perfectly modulated tones and with a pleasant smile.
>
> 'You're sure he's dead?' I said finally.
>
> 'I'm not positive,' she replied uneasily. 'But he was cold. And stiff. And he didn't breathe at all.'
>
> 'That should cover it,' I said.

The tone is immediately recognizable: laconic, wise-ass, laid-back. Grafton's plots, she claimed, usually came from the local newspaper. Living as she did in Santa Barbara (Santa Teresa in her books) the extremes of wealth and poverty are very great. But the motivation for crime in either milieu is always the same: money, power, sex, revenge.

Why do I read so many detective novels? I can console myself with the fact that 50 million copies of Grafton's books have been sold, so I am not alone in needing this particular fix. But I bristle when people dismiss them as mere genre fiction and then invoke the shade of Jane Austen. Only detective fiction! Only first-class writing, wit, originality and deft plotting! But even more than this: a battle is being fought in her books, between good and evil. The arena is recognizably our world, where people are randomly killed and justice is by no means a certainty. As Grafton herself puts it: 'In however a formulaic way, the world of the Private Eye offers up containment and hope and the belief we all have to grimly hold on to: the belief that the individual can make a difference.'

What does any child in a chaotic and disordered household long for? Regular meals, ideally not always cooked by yourself, clean clothes and some sense of order. And when it dawns that it isn't going to happen, perhaps this idea grows instead: it has to be me. I can be the one in charge. The one who creates order. The one who says what's right and wrong. And enforces it. Twenty-five times in fact. So you can say that, in every sense, on my watch, people don't get away with murder.

And we're grateful for it.

FRANCES DONNELLY lives on the Norfolk/Suffolk border where she still bakes cakes.

The Next Bob Dylan

LAURENCE SCOTT

North London, 1966. No time to lose. I bunked off school, withdrew all the money from my Post Office savings account and took a 29 bus to Denmark Street in Soho, where I bought an acoustic guitar and a book called *Play in a Day: Bert Weedon's Guitar Guide to Modern Guitar Playing*. It said in the Introduction that it would enable me to play 'simple vocal accompaniments' and, at 5 shillings, that would do very nicely.

The cause of this sudden depletion in my net worth had occurred the previous afternoon. I'd cycled home from school to find my mother and father in their armchairs waiting for my arrival. She was tearing pages from last week's *Radio Times*, scrunching them up and tossing them into the kindling box, while he drew on his unlit briar. I took a seat on the sofa and prepared for the worst.

'You are now 16 years of age,' my father said. 'In a few weeks you will walk out through your school gates for the last time.' There followed a comprehensive litany of my scholastic failures, rounded off with, 'Your mother and I are concerned about your future.'

They were right to be concerned. Unless it was a fact about cars or my favourite American thriller, or anything whatsoever to do with Shelagh Spaul in Form Five and my unrequited longings, it was most likely to sink in but never resurface. Consequently I came bottom of the class in everything. I coped by developing a nice line in role-play and by pretending to myself that I had exceptional hidden talents

Play in a Day: Bert Weedon's Guitar Guide to Modern Guitar Playing (1957)
Faber · Pb · 44pp · £9.99 · ISBN 9780571529650

and could, whenever I chose, become a Nobel-winning novelist, say, or a jet-setting musician, or an artist living in the south of France *avec* lovers and *châteaux.*

Fortunately, I had recently sat through an entire sixth-form production of *The Winslow Boy* so I knew how to handle parental interrogation. I rose to my feet, put my hands behind my back and strolled to and fro in front of the hearth. 'You needn't worry, Father,' I said. 'I have given my future considerable thought and you will be pleased to hear that I have found a solution which means I shall never have to work for a living.'

My mother paused mid-rip; my father, never one to waste words, struck a Swan Vesta and let his pipe do the talking. I reached into the blue-grey cloud, found his shoulder and placed a comforting hand upon it. 'You see,' I said, 'I am going to be the next Bob Dylan.'

Now, in addition to those difficulties you may already have considered, this particular route to my future wealth and happiness had three major drawbacks: 1. the nearest I'd ever been to a guitar was standing next to Hank Marvin in a lift; 2. my only experience of singing in public was during school assemblies where the works of Marcel Marceau were a particular inspiration; and 3. my sole musical accomplishment was the first three notes of a blues harmonica riff acquired one wet weekend from a Howlin' Wolf LP.

In 1950 guitars were rare in the UK and sales barely touched 5,000, but Elvis, Cliff and British rock 'n' roll changed all that. In 1957, when *Play in a Day* was first published, annual UK guitar sales topped a quarter of a million and the number of people wanting to learn the guitar vastly outnumbered those capable of teaching it – a situation well understood by Bert, who wrote in his Introduction that he wanted his book to contain 'the essential requirements of the lone student without a teacher'. It went straight to the top of the bestseller list and stayed there for several months. With sales to date totalling around 4 million, *Play in a Day* is the world's biggest selling guitar tutor and it's never been out of print.

Like all great delusionists, I had studiously avoided any situation that might expose my pretence, so the physical presence of guitar and teaching manual in my bedroom caused a rush of anxiety. Rather than running my fingers over the guitar's component parts or actually reading the book, I daydreamed my future self into the Albert Hall where I was centre-stage, white-suited and adored by an audience of thousands.

The following morning I discovered that my copy of *Play in a Day* had just 36 stapled pages, no spine, prioritized illustration over text, measured 8½ x 11 inches and was more like a children's comic than a book – an astute combination for a target market of Bert's juvenile fans.

And Bert knew about fans. Before Elvis and Cliff had cut their first records he was already a household name. Born in East London in 1920 to a working-class family, he got his first guitar when he was 12; at 14 he formed his first dance band, and by the 1950s he had become a radio and television regular and the session guitarist of choice for Judy Garland and Frank Sinatra when they were recording in London. For sales of his own recordings of solo guitar music he was awarded gold and platinum discs.

The book's content was divided into two sections. The first included headings such as GUITARS: 'two types, the Cello-built and the Spanish'; PLECTRUMS: 'held in the right hand . . . but don't grip it tightly as this tends to make the fingers and wrist tense'; and HOW TO HOLD THE GUITAR: 'The beginner should sit down at first, only after he has mastered the art can he then think about showmanship and adopt the standing style.' There was also, under HINTS AND TIPS, a harrowing insight into electric guitars of the 1950s: 'Have a chat with an electrician re the earthing of an amplifier as several players have had severe electric shocks.'

The second section was much longer and was primarily concerned with rudimentary musical notation and what to do with your fingers. Apparently, the key to it all was something called a 'chord shape'. Each shape had a name, e.g. D minor, G seventh, A major, and each came with its own explanatory black-line diagram.

'Nature did not fashion our fingers for guitar-playing specifically,' writes Bert – a statement I quickly discovered to be a euphemism. Guitar-playing is *painful*. I was required to stretch and contort my left hand and also endure the pain of steel strings pressing into the soft flesh of my fingertips. Once the left hand was in position I could then pass the plectrum, held in my right hand, across each string in turn and sound something called C major. My efforts were barely audible, episodic, and stumbled into being. Nevertheless, there I was playing the guitar just as Bert had promised – in a day.

I immediately put in place a regular daily routine: at breakfast I positioned *Play in a Day* on the table above my plate, put the guitar across my thigh and, between mouthfuls, practised some of the sixty or more chord shapes chosen by Bert. Ditto lunch and dinner. During the evening while watching television *en famille* I provided simple vocal accompaniments to Reginald Bosanquet on *News at Ten*; and at weekends added harmonic invention to *Sing Something Simple*, my father's favourite music radio programme. I made rapid progress until both book and guitar went missing. I was heartbroken and remained inconsolable for several hours until my mother persuaded my father to give them back.

So certain was I that fame, wealth and assorted *châteaux* would soon be within my grasp, I telephoned my father's younger brother who had contacts with the Unity Theatre Folk Club in Camden Town, and suggested he book me a performance slot so I could make my début to a waiting world. Unfortunately, I had no idea that the Unity was regarded by many as London's premier folk venue and frequented by a notoriously demanding audience.

The club turned out to be a large, packed ground-floor room, smoke-filled, with a bar to one side. Black polo-necks and ripped denim were everywhere; I had a fleeting doubt about the blazer I was wearing – the royal-blue one with brass buttons my mother had spent the afternoon polishing.

Several performers preceded me. All were male, all had rugged, weather-worn faces, colourful neckerchiefs and deep-set eyes which they either closed for added intensity or opened and directed upward for angelic assistance. All sang unaccompanied, and all sang exquisite and poignant songs about the search for love inside factories, the search for love outside factories, and the search for love in the general vicinity of industrialized regions – a mysterious activity requiring a cupped hand behind one ear.

I move my chair to the front of the performing space, sit down and begin to position my fingers one string at a time. I strike my opening chord and sing the first line, 'If you hear the train I'm on . . .' which the cognoscenti recognize immediately as my version of the Peter, Paul and Mary hit single 'Five Hundred Miles' – but it isn't what they want to hear. They want British folk songs sung by servants of the song, not commercial music performed by a schoolboy dressed for a Butlin's talent competition.

I am losing their attention. It is time for added showmanship, but I fail to recall Bert's accompanying caveat *not* to play standing up until you know what you're doing. Consequently, the moment I get to my feet is the moment my playing develops an existential rhythmic complexity that would baffle even John Cage.

My innate inability to apply reason precludes the obvious solution of sitting down again, and suggests that I direct my gaze upwards for angelic assistance. There is none. Instead, I am lifted into another vision of my future self in the Albert Hall: centre-stage and white-suited, only this time I am holding *Play in a Day* in one hand while running the fingers of the other over the component parts of Shelagh Spaul – a vision quickly punctured by the noise of the audience applying their own standing style as they rush to the bar. The once-packed room in Camden Town has suddenly morphed into a saloon on the *Marie Celeste* – a ghostly, smoke-hazed void of deserted tables and chairs. Alone and failing, my guitar is still, and the lyrics dry in my throat.

A solitary voice punctures the silence.

Standing at the back of the room, wearing his old Royal Navy duffel coat, my uncle is singing the words I cannot, beckoning me to join in. I return my smarting fingertips to the strings and together we sing the final chorus. 'I'm five hundred miles / I'm five hundred miles away from home.'

It was the only truth I had uttered all evening.

*

Herbert Maurice Weedon, OBE, died aged 91, in Beaconsfield, on 20 April 2012. There were numerous obituaries in the national press, and many statements of gratitude from those considerably more suited to a life in music than I. Eric Clapton, Mike Oldfield, Hank Marvin, Paul McCartney and Mark Knopfler all publicly acknowledged the role of *Play in a Day* when they, too, were on the threshold of their adult lives.

LAURENCE SCOTT lives and writes in south-west Scotland.

Unsung Heroes

ALASTAIR GLEGG

The library at Fonthill Preparatory School was just what I imagined a Gentlemen's Club to be like: shiny brown leather armchairs with velvet cushions, long oak tables, panelled walls, a coal fire in the corner, and windows looking on to the branches of an enormous beech tree. And, of course, books. It was there that I came to know the schoolboy classics of the time: the adventures of Biggles, the misadventures of William, and the voyages of the Swallows and the Amazons.

Masters would occasionally wander in and out, and it was not until years later that I realized they were not only doing their duty rounds but also guiding young readers to other authors: 'Have you tried this one? Or this one?' Why else would I have bothered to pick out those shabby, dog-eared old volumes? But the people and places discovered in the pages of Robert Louis Stevenson, Walter Scott, G. A. Henty, Jules Verne, H. G. Wells, Rider Haggard, Talbot Baines Reed and many others became part of my world as the wintry wind rattled the windows and the fire sank into glowing embers. There were other territories to explore as well: huge red volumes of *Chums* and *The Boys' Own Paper*, crammed with cricketing heroes and gallant midshipmen; leather-bound copies of the *Illustrated London News* sprinkled with strategic maps of the Battle of the Somme; dozens of volumes of *Punch* decorated with the cartoons of George du Maurier, with brief explanations for those who did not get the joke – *Collapse of stout party!*

There were more recent heroes to read about as well. We were born in the Blitz and we grew up with gas masks: we had no doubts about the rightness of our cause. Most of our schoolmasters had served in the armed forces, although they did not talk about it much, and titles such as Major and Wing-Commander were only attached to their names for a few solemn minutes on Armistice Day. The classic war stories were beginning to appear, and we identified with the real-life heroes of *The Dam Busters*, *Reach for the Sky* and *The Wooden Horse*, and their fictional counterparts in *The Cruel Sea* (only permitted in the bowdlerized 'Cadet Edition' with the swear words and sexual references prudently purged).

But it was in the form-rooms that I began to appreciate the sounds and rhythms of language: not, at first, in English classes, but up several flights of stairs in Mr Storey's cluttered little kingdom. Jammed uncomfortably into ink-stained and battle-scarred desks we were introduced to the intricacies of Latin grammar using, as generations of schoolboys had done before, Kennedy's *Shorter Latin Primer*, first published in 1866. It must be one of the few books in which the Appendix is better remembered than the actual content, because it is there that are found the 'Memorial Lines on the Gender of Latin Substantives'. These were universally known as 'The Jingles', so we missed the mild Victorian pun in the original title. We were required to learn them by heart because (as the Reverend Benjamin Kennedy wisely realized) although learning the rules of grammar is inevitably tedious, the process can be eased by rhythm and verse:

> Masculine are fōns and mōns,
> Chalybs, hydrōps, gryps, and pōns,
> Rudēns, torrēns, dēns, and cliēns,
> Fractions of the ās, as triēns . . .
>
> Fillet of a fenny snake,
> In the cauldron, boil and bake . . .

The last two lines may have been written by somebody else. That does not matter. They are all memorable, and they made me aware that words are not just there to tell a story but can speak for themselves.

Our English master, Mr Stawt, was clearly of that mind, as he introduced us to poetry through verses that appealed to schoolboys who would much rather be running around outdoors. We learned not sonnets or haikus, but poems which cantered and galloped in our heads, like those of Sir Walter Scott:

Young Lochinvar is come out of the west,
Through all the wide border his steed was the best;

and, more dramatically, Lord Byron:

The Assyrian came down like the wolf on the fold,
And his cohorts were gleaming in purple and gold;
And the sheen of their spears was like stars on the sea,
When the blue wave rolls nightly on deep Galilee.

Most especially I remember Don John's approaching army in Chesterton's *Lepanto* – at first just a heartbeat in the distance:

Dim drums throbbing, in the hills half heard . . .

then reaching a crescendo as my fingers tapped the tempo of the drumbeat on the desk:

Stiff flags straining in the night-blasts cold
In the gloom black-purple, in the glint old-gold,
Torchlight crimson on the copper kettle-drums,
Then the tuckets, then the trumpets, then the cannon, and he
    comes.

We were fortunate in having schoolmasters who loved reading and books, and their example fuelled my own growing fascination with words. Mr Kingsley Storey and Mr Michael Cooper, however, stand head and shoulders above the others because they read to us. On

John Tenniel

seemingly endless June evenings, when we had to go to bed long before it was dark, Mr Storey, Head of Classics, would stand in the doorway of one dormitory so that he could be heard in others down the corridor and read aloud. He was a good reader, and through him we became familiar with some of the great works of children's literature. He read us *Alice's Adventures in Wonderland* and *Through the Looking-Glass*, *The Jungle Books* and the *Just So Stories*; he read us Elizabeth Goudge's *The Little White Horse*, and one memorable week he read (and sang) *The Mikado*. He was a tall, slight, rather untidy man with reddish hair, but he managed to conjure up the Wandering Minstrel, the Three Little Maids and the Lord High Executioner as evening shadows lengthened across our iron bedsteads.

Mr Cooper, our History Master, had very different ideas about literature. While I associate Mr Storey's readings with summertime, Mr Cooper's took place by winter's firelight. Once a week or so half a dozen of the older boys were invited down to the sanctuary of the Masters' Common Room after the younger boys had gone to bed. In our dressing gowns and slippers we scurried down the draughty stairs and passages and sat on the worn carpet round the little coal fire, by the light of which Mr Cooper would read aloud from his armchair as he puffed on his pipe, and his fat black cat purred on his lap.

He read us *The Thirty-Nine Steps* and *Greenmantle*; he kept us enthralled with the adventures of Sapper's *Bulldog Drummond*, although the trip back upstairs in the dark was long and scary after a chapter or two of *The Island of Terror*. Most memorably he introduced us to the terrifying ghost stories of M. R. James: one of these tells of a man on holiday who finds an old silver whistle. The whistle summons the wind, which batters at his hotel window to get in, and when it finally succeeds, it makes itself a body out of the sheets on the empty bed next to him, a body with an 'intensely horrible face of crumpled linen'. It was a windy November night when Mr Cooper read us that story, and the clouds were shuttering across the moon. It was not until I had made my nervous way back to a chilly bed and pulled the blankets up around my ears that I realized the bed next to mine was empty – its usual occupant was in the Sick Bay. I didn't sleep much that night.

My family moved to Africa after I left Fonthill, and I never saw any of my former schoolmasters again. It was not until many years later that I realized how much they had taught me over and above their classroom responsibilities, but by then it was too late to say thank you. They had taught me to read, and it is no coincidence that among the hundreds of books that overflow my shelves are those I have mentioned here. There is one other book which I have always associated with Fonthill. When I first read *Stalky & Co.* I naturally set it in a familiar place, a boarding-school I knew very well, and I transposed Stalky, McTurk and Beetle with their escapades to the classrooms, corridors, dormitories and playing fields of my own prep school. There were not really many similarities, I know, but Kipling's tribute to his schoolmasters may serve to express my own gratitude:

> 'Let us now praise famous men' –
>   Men of little showing –
> For their work continueth,
> And their work continueth,
> Broad and deep continueth,
>   Greater than their knowing!

This article was joint winner of our 2018 Writers' Competition. ALASTAIR GLEGG lives on Vancouver Island. He has written articles on the history of education but is actually happier composing limericks and other rude verses which his wife usually forbids him to distribute.

Rudyard Kipling

Bibliography

Svetlana Alexievich, *The Unwomanly Face of War*; *Boys in Zinc*; *Chernobyl Prayer: A Chronical of the Future*; *Second-Hand Time: The Last of the Soviets*   56

Anon., *Sir Gawain and the Green Knight*   34

Alan Bennett, *The Uncommon Reader*   25

Lionel Davidson, *Kolymsky Heights*   41

Charles Dickens, *Barnaby Rudge*   7

Elizabeth Goudge, *The Little White Horse*; *Linnets and Valerians*   68

Sue Grafton's Kinsey Millhone Alphabet novels   79

Elizabeth Jenkins, *Virginia Water*; *Harriet*; *The Tortoise and the Hare*; *Brightness*; *Dr Gully's Story*; *A Silent Joy*; *The View from Downshire Hill*   62

Michael Morpurgo, *War Horse*; *Why the Whales Came*; *Kensuke's Kingdom*; *Private Peaceful*   52

Charles Palliser, *The Quincunx*   74

E. H. Shepard, *Drawn from Memory*; *Drawn from Life*   13

Nan Shepherd, *The Living Mountain*   29

Jeremy Treglown (ed.), *The Letters of John Wilmot, Earl of Rochester*   46

Bert Weedon, *Play in a Day*   83

Virginia Woolf, *The Common Reader*   19

With over 17 miles of open shelves, over one million books to borrow and access to a host of electronic resources, *Slightly Foxed* readers seeking a place to read, write and relax need look no further than The London Library!

Now offering readers £50 off membership for a limited time only.

londonlibrary.co.uk/slightlyfoxed